Increasing
Diversity
in Gifted Education

T0386603

A CEC-TAG Educational Resource

Increasing Diversity in Gifted Education

Research-Based Strategies for Identification and Program Services

Monique T. Felder, Ph.D.,
Gloria D. Taradash, Ph.D.,
Elise Antoine, Mary Cay Ricci,
Marisa Stemple, and Michelle Byamugisha

Series Editors
Cheryll M. Adams, Ph.D., Tracy L. Cross, Ph.D.,
Susan K. Johnsen, Ph.D., and Diane Montgomery, Ph.D.

Routledge
Taylor & Francis Group

NEW YORK AND LONDON

Library of Congress Cataloging-in-Publication Data

Felder, Monique T.
 Increasing diversity in gifted education : research-based strategies for identification and program
services / by Monique T. Felder, Ph.D., Gloria D. Taradash, Ph.D., Elise Antoine, Mary Cay Ricci, Marisa
Stemple, and Michelle Byamugisha.
   pages cm
 ISBN 978-1-61821-270-2 (pbk.)
1. Gifted children--Education--United States. 2. Gifted children--United States--Identification. 3.
Minorities--Education--United States. 4. Children with disabilities--Education--United States. 5. Children
with social disabilities--Education--United States. 6. Educational equalization--United States. I. Title.
 LC3993.F38 2014
 371.95--dc23
                              2014017557

First published in 2015 by Prufrock Press Inc.

Published in 2021 by Routledge
605 Third Avenue, New York, NY 10017
2 Park Square, Milton Park, Abingdon, Oxon OX14 4RN

Routledge is an imprint of the Taylor & Francis Group, an informa business.

Copyright © 2015 by Taylor & Francis Group

Cover and layout design by Raquel Trevino

ISBN: 9781032141701 (hbk)
ISBN: 9781618212702 (pbk)

DOI: 10.4324/9781003235767

Table of Contents

Introduction

Demographics are quickly changing across the United States. According to the 2010 Census (Mackun, Wilson, & Fischetti, 2011), the population of the United States increased from 281.4 million people to 308.7 million people in the last decade. The overwhelming majority of the 27.3 million population increase represents non-White races/ethnicities. Not surprisingly, the Brookings Institution reported that a multiethnic minority student population will continue to pour into America's elementary, middle, and high schools in the coming decades and most likely will become the majority by 2043 (Frey, 2011). The leaders of the 21st century are embodied in that population of culturally, linguistically, and/or ethnically diverse (CLED) students who are rapidly increasing in American public schools; leaders of the 21st century are also embodied in the population of learning disabled students in our public schools. Individuals with exceptional potential, who have been provided with the opportunity to maximize their potential, have made significant contributions to all aspects of American society. This potential is most often cultivated and supported in programs and services for the gifted. However, nationwide, gifted students who are CLED and/or have a disability are systematically underrepresented in programs and services for the gifted (National Association for Gifted Children [NAGC] & Council of State Directors of Programs for the Gifted [CSDPG], 2011). Ford (2014a) used the Relative Difference in Composition Index to statistically analyze the underrepresentation of African Americans and Hispanics in gifted education. She found that as of 2009 and 2011, at least half a million African American and Hispanic students combined were not identified as gifted.

As the field of gifted education considers America's changing demographics and future, the continuing underrepresentation of CLED and twice-exceptional students receiving educational services for the gifted and talented must be addressed. The Association for the Gifted (TAG), a division of the Council for Exceptional Children, embraces diversity as the foundation for developing effective practices to identify and serve children of potential equitably. To that end, TAG developed the document, *Diversity and Developing Gifts and Talents: A National Call to Action* (2009). This document demands a radical change in the way the field of education views and serves gifted children who are culturally, linguistically, and ethnically diverse; who are raised in poverty; who are of diverse sexual orientation; and who are twice-exceptional. The precepts in this document support the actions of TAG.

Gifted education in the 21st century embodies the ideal that the capacity for exceptional achievement exists across all racial, ethnic, language, and economic groups as well as some categories of disability (TAG, 2009). Understanding that ideas of capability change as society evolves, how do we, as practitioners and professional development personnel, answer the call to action? Can we recognize the hints and clues of potential in CLED students as well as students in categories of disability such as those who are twice exceptional? What do we need to know and do to educate diverse and twice-exceptional children at the edge of their ability?

Ford (2010, 2014b) submitted that as professionals prepare to equitably educate culturally different gifted students, that preparation must be grounded in understanding how to create culturally responsive classrooms. Included in that preparation is a critical analysis and professional response to the following three issues (Ford, 2010):

- *Deficit thinking*: Thinking grounded in the belief that culturally different students are genetically and culturally inferior to White students. A belief that their culture—beliefs, values, language, practices, customs, traditions, and more—are substandard, abnormal, and unacceptable.

- *Colorblindness (culture-blindness)*: Intentionally or unintentionally suppressing the importance of and role of culture in learning, curriculum, instruction, assessment, and expectations. A presentation of fairness by not seeing differences and treating everyone the same.
- *White privilege*: Unearned benefits that advantage Whites while disadvantaging others. A form of entitlement and affirmative action in which the social and cultural capital of White Americans is valued and held as normal, normative, or the standard, conferring dominance to one group (p. 32).

This book begins with an overview of issues related to the identification of CLED populations as gifted and talented in Chapter 1. Chapters 2, 3, and 4 each focus on a specific CLED population (i.e., African American students, Hispanic/Latino students, and English language learners). Chapter 5 focuses on twice-exceptional learners. Each of these chapters includes characteristics and research-based best practices. We conclude with the voices of teachers presenting their actual experiences working with gifted CLED students (Chapter 6) and the story of one CLED student's challenges and triumphs in a program for gifted students (Chapter 7). It is important to note that this book was written for practicing professionals (i.e., teachers, school-based and central office administrators, specialists, and counselors) who are responsible for identifying students as gifted and talented and/or planning gifted education programming. Each chapter stands on its own. In other words, it is not necessary to read the entire book to gain information about a specific CLED population or the twice-exceptional learners addressed in this book. For example, if you only want to focus on twice-exceptional learners, you need only to turn to Chapter 5 to learn more about this group of students. Additionally, each chapter on CLED as well as the chapter on twice-exceptional students follows the same format:

- characteristics;
- obstacles to gifted identification;
- best practices for gifted identification;
- concluding remarks; and
- references.

Two appendices are also included. Appendix A provides several resources we've found helpful for teachers of CLED gifted students, particularly in identifying these students. Appendix B includes a copy of the survey we sent out to teachers of CLED students, referenced in the text for Chapter 6.

Although the length of each chapter varies, some information overlaps across chapters, and information on addressing the challenges impacting the identification of a gifted CLED population found in one chapter (i.e., Chapter 4: Gifted English Language Learners) may also be applicable for addressing the challenges of gifted identification for another CLED population (i.e., Chapter 2: Gifted African American Learners), it is important to note that this book was not intended to be all-inclusive or exhaustive. As our reference lists indicate, there is a wealth of additional information available in the field regarding the topics addressed in each chapter of this book. We encourage you to go beyond the pages of this book in your quest to increase your knowledge and understanding about CLED gifted and twice-exceptional students. Our goal was simple—to provide busy educators with the most salient information about each of the CLED populations and twice-exceptional learners discussed in this book. It is our sincere desire that the book's format is found to be practitioner-friendly and that this book provides practitioners with the information and knowledge needed to increase the identification of CLED and twice-exceptional students for gifted education programs and provide services that address their needs.

REFERENCES

Ford, D. Y. (2010). Culturally responsive classrooms: Affirming culturally different gifted students. *Gifted Child Today, 33*(1), 50–53.

Ford, D. Y. (2014a). Segregation and the underrepresentation of Blacks and Hispanics in gifted education: Social inequality and deficit paradigms. *Roeper Review, 36,* 143–145.

Ford, D. Y. (2014b). Why education must be multicultural: Addressing a few misperceptions with counterarguments. *Gifted Child Today, 37*(1), 59–62.

Frey, W. (2011). *America's diverse future: Initial glimpses at the U.S. child population from the 2010 census*. Retrieved from http://www.brook ings.edu/research/papers/2011/04/06-census-diversity-frey

Mackun, P., Wilson, S., & Fischetti, J. (2011). *Population distribution and change: 2000–2010*. U.S. Department of Commerce, Economics and Statistics Administration, U.S. Census Bureau. Retrieved from http://books.google.com/books?id=_7IxtwAACAA J&dq=Mackun+%26+Wilson&hl=en&sa=X&ei=GMBdUquALof G4AORqYGgCA&ved=0CDgQ6AEwAQ

National Association for Gifted Children, & Council of State Directors of Programs for the Gifted. (2011). *2010–2011 State of the states in gifted education: National policy and practice data*. Washington, DC: Author. Retrieved from https://collaborate.education.purdue. edu/edst/gentry/EDPS%20631/State%20of%20States%202010-2011%20(final).pdf

The Association for the Gifted, Council for Exceptional Children. (2009). *Diversity and developing gifts and talents: A national call to action*. Arlington, VA: Author.

CHAPTER I

Overview of Gifted Identification Issues Related to Students from Culturally, Linguistically, and/or Ethnically Diverse (CLED) Backgrounds and Those With Disabilities

"Some of the attitudes that create barriers are things like poor kids and gifted programs just don't go together. I mean, I think that people in their heart of hearts really think that when kids are poor they can't possibly perform at the level of kids that are advantaged because they haven't had certain kinds of advantages in their home."—Dr. Mary Frazier (Grantham, 2002, p. 50)

IDENTIFICATION

The definition of giftedness adopted by a school district delineates the first entry point to gifted identification and placement. Definitions of giftedness and state plans, which outline the criteria to qualify for gifted programs and services, are developed by various entities. They may be written by the state legislatures, state departments of education, the state boards of education, or a body named to address education issues. According to the National Association for Gifted Children and Council

DOI: 10.4324/9781003235767-1

of State Directors of Programs for the Gifted's (NAGC & CSDPG, 2013) 2012–2013 *State of the Nation in Gifted Education: Work Yet to be Done* report, although half (i.e., 27 out of 47) of the states reported more inclusive definitions, only five states included culturally/ethnically diverse populations and only five included gifted students from low-socioeconomic (SES) backgrounds in their definition of gifted. A mere three states included English language learners, and a disappointing two included gifted students with disabilities (NAGC & CSDPG, 2013). As school systems develop their plans for identifying and serving gifted and talented students, care must be taken to be inclusive of *all* populations. Additionally, all pertinent materials must be accessible. For instance, Texas ranks second in Hispanic/Latino population size and the *Texas State Plan for the Education of Gifted/Talented Students* (Texas Education Agency, 2009) is printed in both English and Spanish in the same booklet.

The definition of giftedness that has been most widely adopted by states was issued in the Marland Report (Marland, 1972), which defined gifted children as those capable of high performance, including those with demonstrated achievement and/or potential ability in any of the following areas (singly or in combination): general intellectual ability, specific academic aptitude, creative or productive thinking, leadership ability, visual and performing arts, and psychomotor ability. The United States Department of Education, Office of Educational Research and Improvement (1994), expanded the definition of gifted to include children who show potential for remarkably high levels of accomplishment when compared with others of their age, experience, or environment. The criteria of showing potential for high levels of accomplishment increased the opportunity to include more CLED students. Although most states have adopted a broad definition of giftedness, few actually identify or serve students in all areas.

Exclusive definitions of gifted and talented students or those that focus on only one area of giftedness can be unsuitable for use when identifying CLED students, students in some categories of disability, and students from low-SES backgrounds. Each culture defines giftedness in its own likeness or based on its own image; hence, giftedness in one culture may be expressed differently from giftedness in another culture.

Addressing the challenges of identification can be even more complex when a student is a recent immigrant. When seeking to identify recent immigrants who may be gifted, educators need to have knowledge of linguistic and cultural backgrounds, sociocultural peer-group expectations, cross-cultural stress, intergenerational conflict and attitudinal factors to support effective identification practices (Harris, 1993). Assessment of teacher awareness of immigrant issues and hardships and providing regular opportunities for conversations regarding the implications of negative attitudes and possible biases with teachers are suggested areas of focus for professional development (Harris, 1993; Harris, Guenther, Rosemarin, & Eriksson, 2009).

All children come to the classroom shaped by a myriad of cultural and social influences. Yet, "most schools are middle-class systems that operate from middle-class values" (Slocumb & Payne, 2000, p. 28). Just talking about differences remains an uncomfortable proposition for professionals and laypersons (Ford, 2010). As a result, most school systems use teacher surveys and other subjective performance indicators based on middle-class norms and values as part of their gifted and talented identification and programming processes. Environmental factors such as poverty are typically not considered. Understanding issues of poverty should be central in the gifted and talented identification and programming process, as some immigrant and CLED students may come from low-SES backgrounds and may not have had the same opportunities as their middle class peers.

Teachers, counselors, and administrators are often the school personnel who refer students for gifted and talented services and provide input for gifted identification processes; yet, too often they are unaware of the characteristics of gifted and talented students with disabilities and those from diverse backgrounds. Teachers who have had training in gifted and talented identification recognize certain behaviors as indicators of potential; however, this training, which has been modified and refined over the decades, typically focuses on behaviors and characteristics of children who are White, middle-class, and without disabilities (Neumeister & Burney, 2011). As school populations have become increasingly diverse through the 1990s, the need for a change in teacher training became apparent. NAGC and The Association for the Gifted, Council for Exceptional

Children (CEC-TAG) also revised their Teacher Knowledge and Skill Standards for Gifted and Talented Education in 2006 to respond to this need for better understanding of diversity. This revision of gifted teacher preparation standards infuses issues of human diversity and its impact on families, communities, and schools throughout the standards.

Increasing the identification and placement of underrepresented minorities and students in some categories of disability such as twice-exceptional students in gifted and talented programming will not automatically create equitable access, participation, or achievement for them. For example, because of cultural differences and their developing language acquisition, English language learners may not display the typical characteristics considered by teachers making referrals for gifted screening (Matthews, 2006, 2014). Behaviors, which may be culturally based, may not be recognized as indicators of academic success. In the chapter on English language learners, cultural bias is examined. Obstacles to identification and suggestions to teachers for best practices are outlined.

Behaviors and characteristics that are recognized in the Hispanic/Latino community as indicators that the child "has something special" may not be recognized at all in the school setting. Immigration concerns may have a smothering effect on demonstration of exceptional potential. The chapter on Hispanic/Latino gifted learners will present research focusing on the effects of community and immigration on identification.

Traditionally recognized definitions of giftedness, singular in nature with a focus primarily on academic intelligence, support identification based on high IQ scores and act as a barrier to diverse gifted learners being identified and reaching their full potential. The awareness of characteristics that may differ from mainstream gifted students can aid in identification. The chapter on African American gifted learners presents practical applications and research-based guidelines to guide culturally sensitive identification.

Twice-exceptional learners can present unique characteristics that may mask their giftedness. There is a need to understand their unique array of strengths and weaknesses. They may possess advanced visual-spatial reasoning ability, problem-solve using images, and think in pictures versus in words. In-depth descriptors of these gifted students are presented. Obstacles to identification are identified and research-based best practices for success using a variety of materials and strategies are also presented. In all of the populations presented in this book, parents play a key role in the referral and identification processes; hence, outreach to parents of diverse gifted or potentially gifted students, including twice-exceptional students, is also critical.

When teachers and other professionals understand the characteristics, strengths, and weaknesses of CLED gifted children as well as the characteristics, strengths, and weaknesses of gifted students with disabilities, they will have established the foundation that supports appropriate identification and service to these groups of students. Professional development that is designed to develop cultural competence and cultural proficiency (Lindsey, Robins, & Terrell, 2003) is a key component in the framework that guides teachers and school leaders to evaluate behaviors using a cultural lens that can reveal the hints and clues of exceptional potential in the CLED student population.

In the 1970s, gifted and talented educators came together to write, speak, and advocate for gifted children—children who were at risk from benign neglect. Through the combined advocacy of the great pioneers in the field, dedicated teachers, and committed parents, children with gifts and talents were recognized and supported as learners with unique needs who had the potential to change society when the path was prepared for them. In the 21st century, that same group commitment and advocacy are necessary to bring about results for another group of gifted children suffering from unrealized potential—gifted and talented students from CLED backgrounds and those with disabilities.

REFERENCES

Ford, D. Y. (2010). Culturally responsive classrooms: Affirming culturally different gifted students. *Gifted Child Today, 33*(1), 50–53.

Grantham, T. (2002). Straight talk on the issue of underrepresentation: An interview with Dr. Mary Frazier. *Roeper Review, 24,* 50–51.

Harris, C. (1993). *Identifying and serving recent immigrant children who are gifted.* ERIC Clearinghouse on Disabilities and Gifted Education.

Retrieved from http://www.gifted.uconn.edu/siegle/tag/Digests/e520.html

Harris, C., Guenther, C., Rosemarin, S., & Eriksson, R. (2009, August). *Gifted immigrants and refugees—The gold unmined.* Presentation at the 18th World Council for Gifted and Talented Children, Vancouver, Canada.

Lindsey, R., Robins, K., & Terrell, R. (2003). *Cultural proficiency: A manual for school leaders.* Thousand Oaks, CA: Corwin Press.

Marland, S. P., Jr. (1972). *Education of the gifted and talented: Report to the Congress of the United States by the U.S. Commissioner of Education and background papers submitted to the U.S. Office of Education,* 2 vols. Washington, DC: U.S. Government Printing Office. (Government Documents, Y4.L 11/2: G36)

Matthews, M. (2006). *Working with gifted English language learners.* Waco, TX: Prufrock Press.

Matthews, M. S. (2014). Advanced academics, inclusive education, and English language learners. In M. S. Matthews & J. A. Castellano (Eds.), *Talent development for English language learners: Identifying and developing potential* (pp. 1–13). Waco, TX: Prufrock Press.

National Association for Gifted Children, & The Association for the Gifted, Council for Exceptional Children. (2006). *NAGC-CEC teacher knowledge and skill standards for gifted and talented education.* Retrieved from http://www.nagc.org.442elmp01.blackmesh.com/sites/default/files/standards/NACG-CEC%20CAEP%20standards%20(2006).pdf

National Association for Gifted Children, & Council of State Directors of Programs for the Gifted. (2013). *2012–2013 State of the nation in gifted education: Work yet to be done.* Washington, DC: Authors. Retrieved from http://www.nagc.org/sites/default/files/Advocacy/State%20of%20the%20Nation.pdf

Neumeister, K., & Burney, V. (2011). *An introduction to gifted education: The complete kit for facilitators, coordinators, and in-service training professionals.* Waco, TX: Prufrock Press.

Slocumb, P., & Payne, R. (2000). *Removing the mask: Giftedness in poverty.* Highlands, TX: aha! Process, Inc.

Texas Education Agency. (2009). *Texas state plan for the education of gifted/talented students* Austin, TX: Author. Retrieved from http://www.tea.state.tx.us/index2.aspx?id=6420

U.S. Department of Education, Office of Educational Research. (1994). *National excellence: A case for developing America's talent.* Washington, DC: U.S. Government Printing Office.

CHAPTER 2

African American Gifted Learners

The academic performance of African American students is a long-standing and ongoing national problem. More than four decades of data indicate that African Americans are among the ethnically diverse students who are not achieving at the same rate as their White, Asian, and more socioeconomically privileged peers (Ford, 2011). When the United States Department of Education collected data on African American students identified for gifted programs in 1996, the data indicated that while African American students comprised approximately 17% of the student population, they made up approximately 8% of the students enrolled in gifted and talented programs. This represented approximately 250,000 African American students who were not being provided the opportunity to participate in programs for the gifted (Ford, 2013; United States Department of Education, 1996). Sixteen years later the data remain relatively unchanged. In 2012, the United States Department of Education Office for Civil Rights reported that African Americans represent 19% of the student population, yet they make up 10% of students participating in gifted programs. These data indicate that African American students continue to be disproportionately underrepresented in gifted programs. Hence, it is no surprise that African American students remain underidentified as gifted and talented and are underrepresented in gifted and talented programs and services (Ford, Harris, Tyson, & Trotman, 2002).

Why are African American students so grossly underidentified and underrepresented in gifted and talented programs and services? Although

DOI: 10.4324/9781003235767-2

more research in this area is clearly warranted, research conducted to date indicates that there are many reasons for these situations. The reasons include: (a) use of a conservative definition of giftedness or definitions that do not include the characteristics of some African American students (i.e., oral tradition—a preference to explain something verbally instead of taking a paper-and-pencil test [VanTassel-Baska & Stambaugh, 2007]); (b) issues with screening and selection processes (e.g., intelligence tests as gatekeepers [Ford, 2013]); (c) issues with school personnel and professional development; and, last but not least; (d) instructional and cultural issues (Ford, 2011, 2013).

CONSERVATIVE DEFINITIONS OF GIFTEDNESS

Traditional definitions of giftedness can be unsuitable for use when identifying some African American students and can act as possible barriers for gifted African Americans to reach their full potential, as traditional definitions tend to: (a) be singular in nature with a focus that is primarily on academic intelligence, (b) support identification based on high IQ scores, and (c) emphasize gifted behaviors and characteristics of White and middle class students. Furthermore, each culture defines giftedness in its own likeness or based on its own image; hence, giftedness in one culture may not be considered gifted in another culture. Therefore, traditional definitions of giftedness may not be inclusive or representative enough to identify gifted African American students. One of the most comprehensive definitions of gifted and talented students comes from the United States Department of Education (2012), which defined gifted and talented students as, "Children and youth with outstanding talent who perform or show the potential for performing at remarkably high levels of accomplishment when compared with others of their age, experience or environment" (p. 4). This is a comprehensive definition because it not only focuses on academic gifts and talents, but it also focuses on social gifts and talents that may be present in a child's life. Additionally, this definition recognizes that while some gifted and talented students may already be performing at remarkably high levels, others may just be showing "sparks" or that they have potential and are capable of developing the ability to perform at high levels. Hence, those students should be identified as gifted and talented, too. Incorporating the characteristics that are based on the values and beliefs of African Americans should also be considered in definitions of giftedness. For example, as previously mentioned, by and large African Americans believe that knowledge can be both gained and transmitted orally based on their rich oral traditions (Ford, 2006, 2011). As a result, an African American student may perform better if assessed orally and could be exasperated by paper-and-pencil assessments. Likewise, some African Americans value their unique expressiveness and therefore might select the more creative and imaginative response option over the less-imaginative correct response (Ford, 2006, 2011). Thus, characteristics that include a respect for oral language and expressiveness could prove to be beneficial for African American students and could increase their participation in gifted programs and services (Ford, 2013).

SCREENING AND SELECTION CHALLENGES

One contributing factor regarding why African American students are often not identified as gifted and are overlooked for gifted programs and services is because school districts place far too much emphasis or weight on a single assessment or intelligence test in their identification policies and procedures. As a result, when African American students' scores fall short of the established cut scores, they are overlooked. What could cause an African American student to have depressed scores on achievement, aptitude, or intelligence tests? One reason may be due to not having access to high-quality and rigorous instructional curriculum, programs, and learning experiences prior to being assessed. Another plausible reason for depressed scores can be attributed to the assessments themselves, as some assessments are not culturally fair (Ryser, 2011). Assessments used as part of the gifted and talented screening and identification processes can be culturally biased because they may be normed on a sample of all or predominately White and middle class students. As Ford (2013) explained,

> The primary argument and/or belief is that persons from backgrounds other than the culture (race and economic class) in which the test was developed and normed will always be penalized; they will likely score lower on the test and, thus, have their opportunities and access limited, as well as face misrepresentation about their abilities and potential as gifted students. (p. 110)

Culturally biased tests should be considered of little value because they are invalid and unreliable (Ford, 2011).

Another gifted and talented screening issue that negatively impacts African American students is the overreliance on too few sources of information such as a teacher referral, an achievement test in math or reading (Ryser, 2011), or a cognitive assessment (Ford, 2013; Harris et al., 2007) instead of using multiple assessments and data sources such as a combination of many, if not all, of the following: performance measures (i.e., math and reading levels); a parent checklist; a teacher checklist; cognitive assessments (both verbal and nonverbal); advocacy from other school professionals (i.e., art teacher, music teacher, physical education teacher, school counselor, administrators, reading specialist, etc.) who may see sparks not seen in the classroom setting; advocacy from other persons outside of the school setting who are familiar with a student (i.e., coach, tutor, mentor, etc.); as well as data that can be gathered from student interviews and perceptual information elicited from peers (Slocumb & Payne, 2000). Furthermore, responsible educators need to be acutely aware that only a finite range of abilities can be assessed using intelligence tests (Ford, 2013). Therefore, relying solely or mostly on intelligence assessments or on a limited number of screening measures is strongly not advised when identifying African American students for gifted programs and services. The opposite should be the norm—the more varied the measures that are utilized in the screening process, the better. There's no such thing as "too many data sources" when trying to uncover the gifted potential of African American and other CLED students.

PERSONNEL AND PROFESSIONAL DEVELOPMENT CHALLENGES

Numerous studies indicate that teacher expectations have a powerful impact on student achievement (Good, 1981; Marzano & Marzano, 2010; National Board of Professional Teaching Standards, 2008; Sorhagen, 2013; Thorndike, 1968). Moreover, research indicates that teachers tend to have lower expectations for African American and poor students than they do for their White, Asian, and more socioeconomically advantaged peers (Harris, 2009; Marzano & Marzano, 2010; Wildhagen, 2012). If teachers already have low expectations for African American students, then it is almost impossible for them to perceive African American students as gifted and refer them for gifted and talented identification, programs, and services.

Typically, teachers, counselors, and administrators are often the school personnel who refer students for gifted and talented services and provide input for gifted identification processes, yet too often they are unaware of the characteristics of diverse gifted and talented learners. For example, some educators view behaviors such as "asks many questions" or "questions the relevance of an assignment" as annoying and disrespectful behaviors instead of the behaviors of students who are seeking meaning in their work, which is a common characteristic of gifted learners. As Ford (2013) noted, "teachers and school personnel frequently emphasize behaviors such as cooperation, independence, motivation, task commitment, high grades, and strong language skills when referring and/or personally identifying gifted students" (p. 88). Additionally, school personnel often lack adequate training and preparation in gifted and talented education, the reliability and validity of screening assessments such as cognitive assessments and IQ tests, the implications of teacher expectations on student achievement, and multicultural education and culturally responsive teaching to effectively recognize the gifts and talents of African American and other CLED students.

INSTRUCTIONAL AND CULTURAL CHALLENGES

Ford (2006, 2010, 2011) suggested that teachers tend to use instructional strategies that are mostly verbal, intangible, and decontextualized, yet many African American students need instruction that is more visual, concrete, and contextualized. Just as African American students' perspectives of school performance and behaviors are products of their culture and life experiences, the same holds true for teachers. In fact, some educators hold racial stereotypes that do not allow them to recognize the likelihood of high ability among African American students (Ford, 2006). Moreover, African American students' cultural differences may clash with those in the mainstream—learning preferences, communication styles, behavioral styles, values, and attitudes. According to Ford (2011), teachers who are not familiar with the African American culture may have a deficit view of African American students. As a result, teachers may misinterpret the behaviors of African American students in the classroom, underestimate African American students' academic abilities, and/or provide inappropriate and inadequate instruction, which may lead to diminished student performance in school. These factors may further support teachers' unwillingness to refer African American students for gifted and talented screening, identification, and programs.

CHARACTERISTICS OF GIFTED AFRICAN AMERICAN LEARNERS

Like other CLED gifted and talented learners, gifted and talented African American students may possess characteristics that may manifest to a greater extent or higher degree than in those students found in the mainstream. Additionally, because teachers are often the persons making referrals for gifted and talented identification and services, they should be keenly aware of the ways in which the following gifted characteristics may manifest themselves to a greater extent in African American students (Ford, 2011):

- high nonverbal fluency and originality;
- high creative productivity in small groups;
- adeptness in visual arts;
- high creativity in movement, dance, dramatics, rhythm, music, and other physical activities;
- highly motivated by games, music, sports, humor, and concrete objects;
- use of rich imagery in language;
- articulateness in role-playing, sociodrama, and storytelling;
- responsive to concrete and kinesthetic learning;
- expressive use of gestures, body language; ability to interpret body language;
- enjoyment of and ability in creative movement, dance, drama, music, and rhythm;
- creativity in artistic and musical expressions;
- best able to solve problems with visual and auditory content;
- have strong memories, spontaneous recall;
- fluency of ideas;
- adept to convergent production/group work;
- resourceful and adaptable;
- strong leadership qualities;
- strong vocabulary;
- asks many questions;
- has his or her own ideas;
- has a keen sense of justice, injustice, and human understanding; and
- makes unusual connections. (p. 14)

Teachers can create a chart with these characteristics, note the names of students demonstrating these qualities and capture related anecdotal information each time these behaviors manifest in the students listed.

OBSTACLES TO IDENTIFYING GIFTED AFRICAN AMERICAN LEARNERS

Challenges that impede the identification of gifted and talented African American students are numerous and some have already been discussed in this chapter including: (a) low expectations that teachers hold for African American students and the negative implications those low expectations have on their achievement (National Board of Professional Teaching Standards, 2008; Sorhagen, 2013); (b) bias in some standardized tests, as items may represent White and middle-class experiences (Ford, 2006, 2011, 2013); (c) depressed scores on standardized assessments (Ford, 2006; Ford, Moore, & Milner, 2005); (d) cultural bias due to negative stereotyping about African American students' academic and intellectual abilities (Singleton, Livingston, Hines, & Jones, 2008); (e) lack of or not enough training and professional development in the following: behaviors and characteristics of gifted and talented African American students, the validity and reliability of assessment instruments (Ford, 2011), lack of multicultural education (Banks, 1993), and the absence of culturally responsive classrooms (Gay, 2010; Ladson-Billings, 1995, 2009); and, (f) the implications of focusing on deficits instead of strengths (Ford, 2006, 2011). Other obstacles that have been identified in the research literature include:

- *The language of screening assessments*: Intelligence and achievement tests, which are frequently used in gifted identification processes are written in the language of the dominant culture—Standard American English (SAE)—yet, some African American students do not speak SAE at home or at school (Day-Vines et al., 2009; Harmon, 2004);

- *Negative attitudes related to test taking*: Given the history of intelligence and achievement tests, African American students may hold negative attitudes toward tests in general, which negatively impact their performance on standardized tests. "African American students' negative perception of achievement and intelligence tests contribute to lowering test-taking motivation, greater anxiety, and poor performance on cognitive ability tests" (Harmon, 2004, p. 24); and

- *Test anxiety:* Some African American students may experience stereotype threat, which is anxiety that comes as a result of not wanting to confirm a negative stereotype about his or her group—in this case, the negative stereotype that African Americans do not test well and are less intelligent than other groups. According to Harmon (2004), students who exhibit test anxiety tend to underperform on assessments and are more likely not to perceive themselves as being able to score well on achievement tests.

Although numerous, none of the aforementioned obstacles are insurmountable, and, if eradicated, would positively change outcomes for gifted African American students.

BEST PRACTICES FOR IDENTIFYING GIFTED AFRICAN AMERICAN LEARNERS

There are many promising practices for identifying gifted students (Johnsen, 2011) and African American students in particular (Reis & McCoach, 2000). Schools and school districts must be proactive and do everything they can to ensure that gifted African American students are identified and provided appropriate services to ensure they reach their full potential. Among the promising practices that can be implemented to reverse underidentification and underrepresentation of gifted African American students are accessing good instruction (Harmon, 2004), using multiple measures in the identification process (Ford, 2006, 2013), and providing professional development for teaching staff and administrators (Ford, 2011; Siegle & Powell, 2004).

ACCESS TO GOOD INSTRUCTION
(DARLING-HAMMOND, 2010; HARMON, 2004)

A high-quality rigorous core instructional program is a fundamental component for ensuring student achievement. As a result, African American students must have access to high-quality education and teachers who have high expectations for them. Like all 21st-century learners, African American students must be given the opportunity to:

- think critically,
- problem solve, and
- engage in metacognitive thinking.

USE MULTIPLE ASSESSMENTS
(FORD, 2006, 2013; REIS & MCCOACH, 2000; RYSER, 2011)

A multitude of assessments should be used when identifying giftedness, intelligence, and potential. Overreliance upon one formal instrument or one source of information such as a teacher referral should be avoided at all costs. Other suggestions include:

- allow for multiple criteria rather than a rigid cutoff score on a particular test;
- use local as well as national norms for standardized instruments, particularly when the local population is substantially different from the national population; and
- include informal measures in the battery of assessments used in the screening processes such as nominations (i.e., teachers, parents, and peers), student interviews and work samples, anecdotal information, rating scales, and checklists/surveys.

PROFESSIONAL DEVELOPMENT FOR TEACHERS AND PARENT TRAINING
(CASTELLANO & FRAZIER, 2011; FORD, 2006, 2011; SIEGLE & POWELL, 2004)

Teachers and other professionals should receive ongoing professional development on recognizing the characteristics of giftedness in CLED students and on using and interpreting multiple identification criteria. Schools should:

- provide teachers with substantive, ongoing preparation in gifted education, cultural diversity, linguistic diversity, and economic diversity;
- train teachers on the implications of teacher expectations on student achievement;
- train teachers on how to create gifted education lessons plans that are multicultural;
- train teachers, administrators, and other school staff on the implications of test reliability, validity, and biases;
- train teachers (and parents) on how to nurture students' giftedness/potential;
- ensure parents are thoroughly informed about all aspects of gifted and talented screening, rescreening, and selection criteria and processes including how to advocate for their student; and
- share screening results with and inform parents of selection outcomes.

USE CULTURALLY SENSITIVE AND NONVERBAL INSTRUMENTS (FORD, 2006, 2013; FORD ET AL., 2005; KAUFMAN, PLUCKER, & BAER, 2008; RYSER, 2011)

Utilizing culturally sensitive/"culture fair"/"culture free" tests of intelligence and achievement to support gifted and talented screening, referral and placement decisions, as well as the use of nonverbal assessments (assessments that enable students to analyze and solve complex problems without relying upon or being limited by language abilities) are strongly encouraged. Other suggestions include:

- create or improve teacher and staff referral forms, checklists, and surveys to ensure they capture the strengths of diverse groups and their characteristics (note that Ford [2013] warned that the creation of checklists and surveys by schools must "have respectable levels of reliability and validity, must include local and cultural norms, and must include characteristics of giftedness and culture among Black and Hispanic students" [p. 90]);
- select the least biased assessment instruments;

- include nonverbal assessments, which remove or reduce the role of language in the content, response, and administration of the assessment; and
- include creativity measures such as the figural tests of the *Torrance Test of Creative Thinking* (Torrance, 1974) to assess the nonverbal and creative abilities of African American students.

These strategies are aligned to the National Association for Gifted Children's policy statement on using assessments to identify gifted students. The statement supports the use of more equitable identification and assessment instruments in gifted screening and selection processes.

EARLY IDENTIFICATION
(FORD, 2006, 2011, 2013; OLSZEWSKI-KUBILIUS & THOMSON, 2010)

Some African American students begin to lose interest in school between second and fourth grade. This is around the same time that many districts begin their gifted and talented screening and identification processes. As a result, school districts should be keenly aware of the following:

- the earlier African American students' gifts and talents can be identified, the more likely they are to receive the supports and services needed to develop to their full potential; and
- the goal should not only be to identify gifted and talented African American students, but also to identify African American students who demonstrate undeveloped potential in specific areas including intellectual, academic, artistic, and leadership domains.

RESCREENING/ALLOW FOR MULTIPLE OPPORTUNITIES FOR REFERRALS
(FORD, 2006, 2013)

African American students should regularly be given opportunities throughout their school years to be reassessed for gifted and talented identification, programs, and services. Schools should:

- establish multiple opportunities for school staff to make gifted referrals; and
- allow families and others who have knowledge of the students and who understand the unique gifts and talents associated with different cultural, ethnic, and linguistic groups to initiate referrals.

GIFTED AND TALENTED EDUCATION COMMITTEES
(CLARENBACH, 2007)

Schools may consider forming a Gifted and Talented Education Committee, made up of a racially and professionally diverse group of professionals, to:

- analyze the multiple data points collected,
- track rates of identification,
- compare and question referral rates between CLED students from high and low-socioeconomic families,
- compare and question referral rates between CLED students and their non-CLED peers, and
- examine profiles of culturally and linguistically diverse students who score high on intelligence tests but low on achievement tests.

GIFTED AND TALENTED MENTORING PROGRAMS
(GRANTHAM, 2004; NEVILLE, TYNES, & UTSEY, 2009)

Mentoring programs can have a profound impact on student achievement. Implementing mentoring programs for African American students can help address some of the socioeducational issues that can act as barriers to their identification and achievement in gifted programs. Socioeducational issues are those key factors that correlate with educational outcomes and that schools cannot control such as family income, parents' level of education, etc. Community members as mentors also can provide an opportunity for African American students to engage with successful individuals and role models in their ethnic group "including African American students who were successful in gifted programs" (Neville, Tynes, & Utsey, 2009, p. 231). Moreover, mentors can also speak with African American students about the benefits and even the challenges of participating in gifted and more rigorous programs and increase "African American students' sense of empowerment, improving their problem-solving and decision-making skills, and clarifying their goals for the future to give them a sense of direction" (Neville et al., 2009, p. 231).

CONCLUSION

Historically, African Americans have been significantly underidentified and underrepresented in programs and services for the gifted. This trend continues in the 21st century. In order to effectively interrupt this trend, best practices that mandate identification policies and processes that enable schools to equitably identify and provide programming for gifted African American and other CLED students must be established. These identification systems should be grounded in an inclusionary belief system and should use a myriad of measurements in the identification process instead of a single cut score or overreliance on a teacher's referral. Educators and parents should be informed on how to recognize giftedness in the African American student population as well as how to advocate in order to help African American gifted students to be identified as gifted and to ensure they receive the level of programs and services essential to reaching their full ability and potential.

REFERENCES

Banks, J. (1993). Approaches to multicultural curriculum reform. In J. Banks & C. Banks (Eds.), *Multicultural education: Issues and perspectives* (2nd ed., pp. 195–214). Boston, MA: Allyn & Bacon.

Castellano, J. A., & Frazier, A. D. (Eds.). (2011). *Special populations in gifted education: Understanding our most able students from diverse backgrounds.* Waco, TX: Prufrock Press.

Clarenbach, J. (2007). All gifted is local. *School Administrator, 64*(2), 16.

Darling-Hammond, L. (2010). Recruiting and retaining teachers: Turning around the race to the bottom in high-need schools. *Journal of Curriculum and Instruction, 4*(1), 16–32.

Day-Vines, N. L., Barto, H., Booker, B., Smith, K., Barna, J., Maiden, B., Zegley, L., & Felder, M. (2009). African American English: Implications for school counseling professionals. *Journal of Negro Education, 78,* 70–82.

Ford, D. (2006). Identification of young culturally diverse students for gifted education programs. *Gifted Education Press Quarterly,* 20(1), 2–4.

Ford, D. Y. (2010). Culturally responsive classrooms: Affirming culturally different gifted students. *Gifted Child Today, 33*(1), 50–53.

Ford, D. Y. (2011). *Reversing underachievement among gifted Black students* (2nd ed.). Waco, TX: Prufrock Press.

Ford, D. Y. (2013). *Recruiting and retaining culturally different students in gifted education.* Waco, TX: Prufrock Press.

Ford, D., Harris, J., III, Tyson, C., & Trotman, M. (2002). Beyond deficit thinking: Providing access for gifted African American students. *Roeper Review, 25,* 52–58.

Ford, D., Moore, J., & Milner, H. (2005). Beyond culture blindness: A model of culture with implications for gifted education. *Roeper Review, 27,* 97–103.

Gay, G. (2010). *Culturally responsive teaching: Theory, research, & practice* (2nd ed.). New York, NY: Teachers College Press.

Good, T. (1981). Teacher expectations and student perceptions: A decade of research. *Educational Leadership, 12*(1), 415–422.

Grantham, T. (2004). Rocky Jones: Case study of a high-achieving Black male's motivation to participate in gifted classes. *Roeper Review, 26,* 208.

Harmon, D. (2004). They won't teach me. *Roeper Review, 24,* 68–75.

Harris, B., Rapp, K., Martinez, R., & Plucker, J. (2007). Identifying English language learners for gifted and talented programs: Current practices and recommendations for improvement. *Roeper Review, 29,* 26–29.

Harris, M. (2009). *Teachers' expectations of middle school students.* Washington, DC: Trinity College.

Johnsen, S. K. (Ed.). (2011). *Identifying gifted students: A practical guide* (2nd ed.). Waco, TX: Prufrock Press.

Kaufman, J., Plucker, J., & Baer, J. (2008). *Essentials of creativity assessment: Essentials of psychological assessment.* Hoboken, NJ: Wiley

Ladson-Billings, G. (1995). But that's just good teaching! The case for culturally relevant pedagogy. *Theory Into Practice, 34,* 159–165.

Ladson-Billings, G. (2009). *The dreamkeepers: Successful teachers of African American children* (2nd edition). San Francisco, CA: Jossey-Bass.

Marzano, J. S., & Marzano, R. J. (2010). The inner game of teaching. In R. Marzano (Ed.), *On excellence in teaching* (pp. 345–367). Bloomington, IN: Solution Tree Press.

National Association for Gifted Children. (2008). *The role of assessments in the identification of gifted students* [Position statement]. Washington, DC: Author. Retrieved from http://www.nagc. org.442elmp01.blackmesh.com/sites/default/files/Position%20 Statement/Assessment%20Position%20Statement.pdf

National Board of Professional Teaching Standards. (2008). *Assessing accomplished teaching: Advanced-level certification programs.* Arlington: VA: Author.

Neville, H. A., Tynes, B. M., &. Utsey, S. O. (2009). *Handbook of African American psychology.* Thousand Oaks, CA: Sage.

Office for Civil Rights. (2012). *The transformed Civil Rights data collection.* Retrieved from http://www2.ed.gov/about/offices/list/ocr/ docs/crdc-2012-data-summary.pdf

Olszewski-Kubilius, P., & Thomson, D. (2010). Gifted programming for poor or minority urban students: Issues and lessons learned. *Gifted Child Today, 33*(4), 58–64.

Reis, S., & McCoach, D. (2000). The underachievement of gifted students: What do we know and where do we go? *Gifted Child Quarterly, 44,* 152–179.

Ryser, G. R. (2011). Fairness in testing and nonbiased assessment. In S. K. Johnsen (Ed.), *Identifying gifted students: A practical guide* (2nd ed., pp. 63–74). Waco, TX: Prufrock Press.

Siegle, D., & Powell, T. (2004). Exploring teacher biases when nominating students for gifted programs. *Gifted Child Quarterly, 48,* 5–17.

Singleton, D., Livingston, J., Hines, D., & Jones, H. (2008). Under-representation of African American students in gifted education programs: Implications for sustainability in gifted classes. *Perspectives, 10*(1). Retrieved from http://www.rcgd.isr.umich.edu/prba/perspectives/spring%202008/Singleton-Livingston-Hines-Jones.pdf

Slocumb. P., & Payne, R. (2000) *Removing the mask: How to identify and develop giftedness in students from poverty.* Highlands, TX: aha! Process, Inc.

Sorhagen, N. (2013). Early teacher expectations disproportionately affect poor children's high school performance. *Journal of Educational Psychology, 105,* 465–477.

Thorndike, R. (1968). Review of Pygmalion in the classroom. *American Educational Research Journal, 102,* 708–711.

Torrance, E. (1974). *Torrance Tests of Creative Thinking.* Bensenville, IL: Scholastic Testing Service.

United States Department of Education. (1996). *Goals 2000: Increasing student achievement through state and local initiatives.* Washington, DC: Author.

Van Tassel-Baska, J., & Stambaugh, T. (2007). *Overlooked gems: A national perspective on low-income promising learners.* Washington, DC: National Association for Gifted Children.

Wildhagen, T. (2012). How teachers and schools contribute to racial differences in the realization of academic potential. *Teachers College Record, 114*(7), 1–27.

CHAPTER 3

Hispanic/Latino Gifted Learners

It is estimated that by 2023, minorities will comprise more than half of all children in America. Although the majority of students are still identified as non-Hispanic White (59%), they are followed by Hispanic/Latino students (18%) and Black students (15%). Collectively, minorities are expected to become the majority by 2043, with the nation projected to be 54% minority by 2050 (Davis & Bauman, 2011). According to 2012 Census Bureau data, Latino children comprise at least 20% of the public school kindergarten population in 17 states including Nebraska, Idaho, Washington, Kansas, and Oregon (Krogstead, 2014). Hispanic/Latino children arrive at school with varying levels of language skills. A term used to describe students whose first language is not English and who are still learning the English language is English Language Learner (ELL). Kitano and Pedersen (2002) found English language learners to be a heterogeneous group reflecting differences in primary language proficiency and in English. In school settings, ELL status is usually determined by a student's score on an English proficiency test (Pereira & Gentry, 2013). Some Hispanic/Latino students will arrive at school as English language learners but that should not be an automatic assumption. This chapter will focus on the characteristics, strengths, and needs of high-ability Hispanic/Latino students, including some aspects of language.

The Hispanic/Latino population is projected to nearly triple, from 46.7 million to 132.8 million during the 2008–2050 period. The Hispanic/Latino share of the nation's total population is projected to

 DOI: 10.4324/9781003235767-3

double, from 15% to 30%. Thus, nearly one in three U.S. residents will be Hispanic (Bernstein & Edwards, 2008).

The definition of Hispanic/Latino origin in this text is taken from the 2010 Census report (Humes et al., 2011): "Hispanic or Latino" refers to a person of Cuban, Mexican, Puerto Rican, South or Central American, or other Spanish culture or origin regardless of race (p. 2). In this chapter, the terms Hispanic and Latino are used interchangeably.

In 2007, almost 34% of the Hispanic/Latino population was younger than 18 (Bernstein, 2008). This growing Hispanic/Latino population is producing a diversity of students who will enter school from many environments including children being raised in the highest income categories, children who are raised in poverty, English language learners, recent immigrants, children in need of remedial services, children with exceptional potential, and children with identified gifts and talents. Individuals with exceptional potential who have been provided with the opportunity to maximize that potential have made significant contributions to all aspects of society (Castellano & Frazier, 2011); hence, this diverse population demands that schools examine their current practices and determine what changes are necessary to identify and serve this population with exceptional potential, including those who are bilingual and English language learners.

CHARACTERISTICS OF HISPANIC/ LATINO GIFTED LEARNERS

Like other culturally diverse school populations, Hispanic/Latino students also are historically underserved in programs providing gifted services. Nationally, Hispanics/Latinos are about 50% less likely than White students to be identified for gifted programs (Naglieri & Ford, 2003). Ford (2013) estimated that this population makes up about 20% of the public school population, but "much less" of the population of gifted programs—based on data from the Office for Civil Rights, she estimated the underrepresentation of this population to be close to 40% (p. 24). Like other CLED students, many Hispanic/Latino students come from backgrounds that differ both culturally and linguistically from

TABLE 4.1
ABSOLUTE ASPECTS OF GIFTEDNESS AND
CONCOMITANT CULTURAL VALUES

Absolute Aspects of Giftedness	Cultural Values Often Characteristic of Hispanics/Latinos	Behavioral Differences
High level of verbal ability	Traditional language of family	Communicates fluently with peers and within community, even if using nonstandard English
Emotional depth and intensity	Abrazo, a physical or spiritual index of personal support	Requires touching, eye contact, feeling of support to achieve maximum academic productivity
Unusual sensitivity to feelings and expectations of others	Family structure and dynamic–male dominance	Personal initiative, independent thought, and verbal aggressiveness often inhibited in females
Conceptualize solutions to social and environmental problems	Nuclear and extended family closeness valued	Often assumes responsibility for family and/or younger siblings
Unusual retentiveness; unusual capacity for processing information	Traditional culture	Adapts to successful functioning in two cultures
Leadership	Collaborative rather than competitive dynamic	Accomplishes more, works better in small groups than individually

Note. From *Critical issues in gifted education: Defensible programs for cultural and ethnic minorities* (Vol. II, pp. 43, 50) by C. J. Maker & S. W. Schiever (Eds.), 1989, Austin, TX: Pro-Ed. Copyright 1989 by Pro-Ed. Reprinted with permission.

those students (i.e., White and middle class) who are typically selected to participate in gifted and talented programs. Given that the Hispanic/Latino community is made up of many different ethnic and cultural groups, educators must examine and understand the many aspects of the Hispanic/Latino culture, family, and community to support equitable referral, identification, and placement in gifted service for those students who show the hints and clues of exceptional potential. Maker & Schiever (1989) presented the absolute aspects of giftedness and the concomitant cultural values in Table 4.1.

It is important for educators to be aware of characteristics demonstrated by Hispanic/Latino students that indicate exceptional potential. In his article on gifted and talented Hispanic students, Castellano (1998) identified the following characteristics as common among gifted Hispanic/Latino students:

- rapidly acquire English language skills once exposed to the language and given an opportunity to use it expressively;
- exhibit leadership ability, although often in an open or unobtrusive manner, with strong interpersonal skills;
- tend to have older playmates and easily engage adults in lively conversation;
- enjoy intelligent and (or effective) risk-taking behavior, often accompanied by a sense of drama;
- can keep busy and entertained, especially by imaginative games and ingenious applications, such as getting the most out of a few simple toys and objects;
- are able to assume high levels of responsibility and will accept responsibilities at home normally reserved for older children, such as the supervision of younger siblings or helping others to do their homework; and
- are "street wise" and are recognized by others as youngsters who have the ability to "make it" in the Anglo-dominated society. (pp. 3–4)

Other researchers and scholars (Castellano, 2004; Esquierdo & Arreguín-Anderson, 2012; Harris, Rapp, Martinez, & Plucker, 2007) have found the following characteristics in gifted Hispanic/Latino students:

- demonstrate well-developed social skills;
- exhibit high sensitivity towards their peers and have good relationships with them;
- have a healthy self-esteem;
- are able to thrive in a variety of settings;
- demonstrate strong social competence;
- are highly motivated to learn and succeed in school;
- are resilient; and
- demonstrate high achievement despite obstacles, adversities, and challenges.

Moreover, bilingual gifted Hispanic/Latino students not only enjoy reading, speaking, listening, and writing in their native language, they may excel in one or more of those areas, too.

Educators should not dismiss these traits as unimportant if they observe them in their Hispanic/Latino students; rather, educators should advocate for Hispanic students demonstrating these traits to be screened and considered for gifted and talented programs and services.

In summary, it is imperative for educators to be knowledgeable of these characteristics and use them to effectively respond to the programmatic and identification needs of gifted Hispanic/Latino students.

OBSTACLES TO IDENTIFYING GIFTED HISPANIC/ LATINO LEARNERS

Researchers and scholars have identified numerous reasons for the underidentification and underrepresentation of Hispanic/Latino and other CLED students in gifted programs. Obstacles identified by researchers that have led to the severe shortage of Hispanic/Latino students identified as gifted and/or who are in gifted programs include deficit thinking, ineffective policies and procedures, ineffective screening instruments, a lack of cultural understanding, and poor school-parent relationships.

DEFICIT THINKING

Ford (2006) identified deficit thinking as one of the primary reasons for the underidentification of Hispanic/Latino and other CLED learners as gifted. Deficit thinking

inhibits individuals [educators] from seeing strengths in people [students] who are different from them; instead, attention centers on what is 'wrong' with the 'different' individual [student] or group [students], having low expectations for them, feeling little to no obligation to assist them, and feeling superior to them. (Ford, 2006, p. 52)

In other words, if educators attribute Hispanic/Latino students' underachievement in school or underrepresentation in gifted programs to something being "wrong" with the students and not, for example, as related to instruction, or to the lack of access to academic opportunities, those educators are far more inclined to have low expectations for those students. Low teacher expectations and beliefs create conditions and a culture that make it virtually impossible for them to refer Hispanic/Latino or other CLED students for gifted identification and/or to advocate favorably for their inclusion in gifted programs (Hughes, 2011).

POLICIES AND PRACTICES

Ineffective policies and procedures are yet another obstacle to adequately identifying gifted Hispanic/Latino learners. One such policy identified by researchers is reliance on teacher referrals in the gifted identification process (Ford, 2006, 2013; Latz & Adams, 2011; Neumeister, Adams, Pierce, Cassidy, & Dixon, 2007; VanTassel-Baska & Johnsen, 2007). In far too many school districts, students cannot be assessed or screened for gifted identification and programs without a favorable recommendation/referral from his or her teacher. Based upon a teacher's beliefs, attitudes, and expectations, he or she can be a gatekeeper or an initiator for the referral of Hispanic/Latino gifted children. As Ford (2013) noted, when teachers' expectations are positive, they are more likely to refer CLED students for gifted programs (conversely, she explained, when their expectations are low, referral is less likely). These beliefs and expectations can be influenced by a child's race, physical appearance, and language use. A study by Carmen (2011) explored the critical issue of teacher stereotyping. She found gifted referrals could be affected by a teacher's perception of a student's race, culture, socioeconomic status, parental education, and single parent status. Primary grade teachers could not readily envision students as gifted who were poor or not white. Even teachers from CLED backgrounds were found to hold stereotypical thoughts (Young, 2010) about their CLED students.

If a teacher has deficit thinking, low expectations for Hispanic/Latino students' achievement, and/or cannot recognize the characteristics of gifted Hispanic/Latino learners, then that teacher is less likely to refer Hispanic/Latino students for gifted screening or programming (Ford,

2013). Educators can begin to address stereotypical beliefs through learning about their students' families and communities, examining their own assumptions about differences and analyzing their expectations (Young, 2010).

Peterson (2006) examined the behaviors of teachers considering potential nominees for gifted programs and found cultural factors may play a role impacting classroom behavior, teacher-student relationships, and students' fit in the school environment. The selection criteria of dominant-culture values such as good behavior, verbal assertiveness, perceived work ethic, social status, and social skills might preclude identification of children from cultures that do not value verbal assertiveness and "standing out," as well as students with low English proficiency, behavior problems, low-socioeconomic status, and poor social skills (Peterson, 2006, p. 44). Teachers must be sensitive to these cultural factors when observing CLED students, giving particular focus to Hispanic/Latino students with intertwining issues of language and social skills.

INEFFECTIVE SCREENING INSTRUMENTS

Another obstacle to identifying gifted Hispanic/Latino learners is the use of ineffective screening instruments. Ineffective screening instruments for identifying minority students are those that are biased toward the mainstream population and are culturally insensitive, which makes them invalid for Hispanic/Latino students. Although the sole or overreliance on any one assessment instrument is strongly discouraged, when used as part of the gifted identification process, it is critical that unbiased and culturally sensitive assessments such as nonverbal tests be used. If not, Hispanic/Latino students will continue to be underidentified and denied access to gifted programs, due to their inability to move beyond the assessment phase of a screening process.

POVERTY AND IMMIGRATION ISSUES

Cultural issues brought about by socioeconomic status can have a profound effect on gifted referral. In 2010, 6.1 million Hispanic/Latino children were living in poverty, more than any other racial or ethnic group (Kochlar, Fry, & Taylor, 2011). However, great caution must be taken not to stereotype all Hispanics/Latinos as low income or in poverty. In the 2005 to 2009 recession, within the Hispanic/Latino community, the top 10% of that community saw a 15% rise in their wealth (Kochlar et al., 2011).

Immigration and poverty often are inextricably linked. Some Hispanic/Latino gifted children in poverty face issues that do not affect American diverse gifted children being raised in poverty. One of the dominant areas of concern for some Hispanic/Latino students and their families is the issue of immigration. Moreover, children with immigrant parents—both documented and undocumented—are the fastest growing segment of the nation's child population. About three quarters (76%) of the nation's unauthorized immigrant population are Hispanic/Latino (Passel & Cohen, 2009). The majority of undocumented immigrants (59%) are from Mexico, numbering 7 million (Passel & Cohen, 2009). The number of families with unauthorized immigrant parents and citizen children numbered 4 million in 2008. A third of these children live in poverty, nearly double the poverty rate for children of U.S.-born parents. These children comprise an increasing share of students in kindergarten through grade 12 (Passel & Cohen, 2009). Many live in homes where no one 14 years of age or older speaks English proficiently—an environment described as linguistically isolated (Fortuny, 2010).

Increased raids and deportation of unauthorized immigrants have led to 40% of Hispanics/Latinos worrying that they themselves, a member of their family, or a close friend will be deported. Counselors report some children of unauthorized immigrants are unable to sleep for fear their home will be raided in the middle of the night. And, some children are kept home for fear of immigration checkpoints at the school. At school, children are reported to be sleepy and unable to concentrate (Orozco & Thakore-Dunlap, 2010). These conditions lead to a suppression of outgoing behaviors and perhaps a diagnosis of remediation while signs of potential are masked.

The guidelines in Figure 4.1 support service and identification of gifted immigrant and refugee populations (Harris, Guenther, Rosemarin, & Eriksson, 2009).

GUIDELINES FOR POPULATIONS OF GIFTED IMMIGRANTS AND REFUGEES IN THE GLOBAL COMMUNITY

1. Involve parents in identification and programming of gifted immigrants and refugees, taking into account individual aspirations.

2. Encourage and maintain sensitivity to cultural differences in staff, school climate, and student peers.

3. Assess the teacher attitudes periodically.

4. Utilize the developmental rather than a crisis-oriented model, or a view that the students are coming with liabilities.

5. Utilize curriculum-based assessment that provides diagnostic information and allows teachers to accommodate instruction with the regular classroom.

6. Promote teacher awareness of the adjustments and hardships some immigrants and refugees must endure.

7. Stay alert to contrasts in economic status that impact self-esteem and provide social assistance to gifted children in immigrant families from deprived areas.

8. Include direct observation in identification procedures to locate the gifted and talented among immigrant families.

9. Utilize high-level values consistently, without regard to economic status and recognize the need to improve the whole education system.

10. Implement community centers in underserved areas and utilize volunteer services wherever possible to fill in service gaps.

11. Multicultural teacher trainers should recognize and address the coexistence of excellence with cultural isolationism in both pre-service and in-service contexts.

12. Utilize mediated learning.

13. Recognize that students may be culturally different rather than culturally deprived.

14. Take into account the probability of incongruence between the previous learning experience and the demands of the new educational system.

15. Emphasize the need to develop core content, skills and higher standards across all levels, particularly in science, mathematics, and language.

16. Place stress on programs that accelerate students and bridge gaps in learning that have stemmed from past inequitable education systems and develop leadership that includes the cultural perspectives of immigrant gifted students.

17. Train teachers in both core content areas and the use of higher level thinking processes to meet objectives of outcomes-based education with strategies appropriate for gifted students.

18. Re-examine the effectiveness of outcomes-based education and teacher training in implementation.

Figure 4.1. Guidelines for populations of gifted immigrants and refugees in the global community. *Note.* From *Gifted immigrants and refugees: The gold unmined* by C. Harris, Z. Guenther, S. Rosemarin, & G. Eriksson, 2009, Presentation at the 18th World Council for Gifted and Talented Children, Vancouver, Canada. Reprinted with permission.

SCHOOL-PARENT RELATIONSHIPS

The school-parent relationship plays a key role in the identification and referral process. Hispanic/Latino parents may bring a different school relationship experience to the referral setting. Limited English proficiency may add to the reluctance some Hispanic/Latino families have to interact with the school. For some parents, interaction with the school has only occurred when there is a problem and therefore the school relationship is to be avoided. Still other parents may see the school and the gifted program as interfering with family by requiring their child to stay after school or attend on Saturday to participate in gifted activities. Additionally, uneducated parents may face the additional obstacle of lacking the skills to advocate for their gifted child when necessary.

School personnel are reported to have difficulty understanding low-income immigrant Hispanic/Latino parents (Orozco, 2008). For example, teachers have reported having little knowledge about how parents with less than a high school education are involved with their children (Baker, Kessler-Sklar, Piotrkowski, & Parker, 1999). When interacting with parents, even the choice of language is important. If a descriptor is necessary, does a teacher refer to the parental status as illegal immigrant, alien, unauthorized, or undocumented? The choice of language can make the child and family members feel welcome or unwelcomed; safe or unsafe. Krugman and Iza (2014) recommended communicating to parents in their language, relying on a fully bilingual interpreter to help teachers in meetings with parents and to translate written information from the school.

BEST PRACTICES FOR IDENTIFYING GIFTED HISPANIC/ LATINO LEARNERS

Continued advocacy for addressing the underidentification and underrepresentation of Hispanic/Latino students with outstanding talents has helped to identify several promising practices that can reverse this trend. One promising practice that educators can implement immediately is to expand their definition of giftedness to ensure it is inclusive of the unique characteristics of gifted Hispanic/Latino children. Esquierdo and Arreguín-Anderson (2012) posited that a definition of giftedness for bilingual and Hispanic/Latino students begins with the Marland Report (Marland, 1972) definition of high performance, demonstrated achievement, and/or potential ability; includes the Office of Educational Research and Improvement (OERI; U.S. Department of Education, 1994) definition of those who show potential for remarkably high levels of accomplishment when compared with others of their age, experience, or environment; and significantly must also be based upon the child's life experiences. Esquierdo and Arreguín-Anderson (2012) supported the position presented by Lara-Alecio and Irby (2000) that bilingual children grow up in a socially, linguistically, and culturally diverse environment and, therefore, giftedness manifests itself differently. To define this difference, Lara-Alecio and Irby begin with Renzulli's (1977) three dimensions of above-average ability, creativity, and task commitment and overlay the application of social, linguistic, and cultural experiences to present a model that helps school personnel understand how to assess behaviors that are shaped by the Hispanic/Latino life experiences of growing up in a diverse environment. Some characteristics of this model include expressive language, cultural sensitivity, family connections, creative performance, and problem solving in a nonhurried manner. This model makes teachers aware of gifted characteristics that are assessed differently when viewed through a cultural lens. For instance, a behavior such as a preference for collaboration may be seen as a lack of leadership skills rather than a highly developed ability to work with others with whom the child may have few shared cultural experiences including language (Esquierdo & Arreguín-Anderson, 2012). The gifted characteristic of keen use of social and academic language is demonstrated by the use of code switching in understanding and applying the nuances of standard and colloquial English and Spanish as well as slang in both languages.

ONGOING PROFESSIONAL DEVELOPMENT

It is important for educators to recognize and appreciate that Hispanic/Latino children, like all other children, come to the classroom shaped by cultural and social influences. Behaviors and characteristics that are recognized in the home community as indicators that the child "has something special" may not be recognized at all in the school setting. Teachers must know and understand the family situation of their Hispanic/Latino students to accurately interpret their behaviors. If Hispanic/Latino children are only a small proportion of an Anglo classroom or are new immigrants in a class of acculturated Hispanic/Latino children, they may feel isolated and may inhibit behaviors that indicate leadership or creativity.

Increased commitment to culturally responsive professional development is another promising practice for increasing the identification of gifted Hispanic/Latino learners. With changing demographics and the diversity of students coming into our schools, the following guidelines will support the identification process for Hispanic/Latino and other CLED students:

- Educators must expand their knowledge, training, and experience until they automatically recognize gifted indicators when observing Hispanic children.
- School faculty, educational staff, and parents must be educated to recognize the signs of giftedness in Hispanic/Latino children.
- The whole school must be charged with the responsibility to search for gifted indicators.
- A clear and simple process for nomination must be in place and easily available (Banda, 1989).

As the entire school community looks for potentially gifted children, Banda (1989) emphasized the importance of instilling an appreciation for the uniqueness, difficulty, and responsibility of being a gifted Hispanic/Latino individual.

Professional development that is designed to develop cultural competence and cultural proficiency (Ford, 2010; Lindsey, Robins, & Terrell, 2003) will help equip teachers and school leaders to evaluate behaviors of gifted Hispanic/Latino learners through a cultural lens. This professional development is enhanced by including all school staff (i.e., professional and supporting) as well as other stakeholders such as parents and family members, community leaders, volunteers, and significant community members.

PARENT ENGAGEMENT AND TRAINING

Engaging and educating parents is yet another invaluable means for ensuring Hispanic/Latino gifted learners are identified and have access to the gifted programs they deserve. In addition to a reluctance to interact with the school, parents of Hispanic/Latino children ask for an evaluation for gifted classes much less often than White parents. Even when the parents are aware of superior abilities in their children, that awareness may not be enough to motivate an active parental role in the referral process. A public education program to inform parents about programs for the gifted would be helpful in developing parent advocacy (Scott, Perou, Urbano, Hogan, & Gold, 1992).

Working with school counselors, educators can inform Hispanic/Latino families about gifted issues. School counselors may be seen as a safe source—someone removed from the person who has control of the child's educational future. Schools can also partner with community-based organizations that have established trust and respect within the community (Van Velsor & Orozco, 2007).

School districts, schools, and organization can support parents of Hispanic/Latino students to understand the value of identifying and placing their child in programs for the gifted by implementing the following strategies recommended by The Center for Comprehensive School Reform and Improvement (Leeks & Stonehill, 2008) and adapted to meet the needs of gifted Hispanic/Latino students:

- translating into native language critical information that the student or family must know about gifted referral and identification;
- explaining how expectations, curriculum, and classroom procedures are designed to help a child reach his or her maximum potential;
- identifying differences in instruction and content from that in the regular classroom;
- explaining how afterschool programs, summer programs, and camps can more rapidly build linguistic, academic, and social skills;
- providing information on classes or training for parents to help their gifted child; and

- providing opportunities for gifted students and families to network with others.

CONCLUSION

The population of students of Hispanic/Latino origin continues to rapidly increase, giving education professionals the unique opportunity to design the structure of the programs that will identify and serve those children who show the potential for exceptional achievement. As the field focuses on this growing population, educators must be aware that Hispanic/Latino origin is not a monolith, and one descriptor that fits all of these gifted children does not exist. Children from Honduras, Cuba, Brazil, or Mexico all bring different cultural experiences that shape the demonstration of their potential. Knowledge of immigrant concerns will also assist educators in understanding behaviors that may be demonstrated when a Hispanic/Latino child with exceptional potential is being raised in poverty or is involved in family issues of immigration. As policies and procedures are designed, professional development will be a critical aspect. Chapter 3 describes the intersection of language in identification. These characteristics are also useful as informational tools for providing services. The impact immigration and poverty may have on these gifted children requires professionals to candidly assess their own belief systems and analyze what may be stereotypical views that would stifle potential. Involving school professionals, family members, and key community members will provide invaluable insight into a population whose potential can be more fully realized when everyone is involved in program development.

REFERENCES

Baker, A., Kessler-Sklar, S., Piotrkowski, C., & Parker, F. (1999). Kindergarten and first-grade teachers' reported knowledge of parents' involvement in their children's education. *The Elementary School Journal, 99,* 367–380.

Banda, C. (1989). Promoting pluralism and power. In C. Maker & S. Schiever (Eds.), *Critical issues in gifted education: Defensible programs for cultural and ethnic minorities, volume II* (pp. 27–33). Austin, TX: Pro-Ed.

Bernstein, R. (2008). *United States Census Bureau Newsroom: U.S. Hispanic population surpasses 45 million now 15 percent of total.* CB08-67. Retrieved from http://www.census.gov/newsroom/releases/archives/population/cb08-67.html.

Bernstein, R., & Edwards, T. (2008). *United States Census Bureau Newsroom: An older and more diverse nation by midcentury.* CB08-123. Retrieved from http://www.census.gov/newsroom/releases/archives/population/cb08-123.html.

Carmen, C. (2011). Stereotypes of giftedness in current and future educators. *Journal for the Education of the Gifted, 34,* 790–812.

Castellano, J. (1998). *Identifying and assessing gifted and talented bilingual Hispanic students.* Charleston, WV: ERIC Clearinghouse on Rural Education and Small Schools. (ERIC Document Reproduction Service No. ED423104)

Castellano, J. (2004). Empowering and serving Hispanic students in gifted education. In D. Boothe & J. C. Stanley (Eds.), *In the eyes of the beholder: Critical issues for diversity in gifted education* (pp. 1–14). Waco, TX: Prufrock Press.

Castellano, J. A., & Frazier, A. D. (Eds.). (2011). *Special populations in gifted education: Understanding our most able students from diverse backgrounds.* Waco, TX: Prufrock Press.

Davis, J. W., & Bauman, K. J. (2011, August). School enrollment in the United States: 2006. *US Census Bureau: Current Population Reports.* Retrieved from http://www.census.gov/prod/2008pubs/p20-559.pdf

Esquierdo, J., & Arreguín-Anderson, M. G. (2012). The "invisible" gifted and talented bilingual students: A current report on enrollment in GT programs. *Journal for the Education of the Gifted, 35,* 35–47.

Ford, D. (2006). Identification of young culturally diverse students for gifted education programs. *Gifted Education Press Quarterly, 20*(1), 2–4.

Ford, D. Y. (2010). Culturally responsive classrooms: Affirming culturally different gifted students. *Gifted Child Today, 33*(1), 50–53.

Ford, D. Y. (2013). *Recruiting and retaining culturally different students in gifted education.* Waco, TX: Prufrock Press.

Fortuny, K. (2010). *Five questions for Karina Fortuny on children of immigrants.* Retrieved from http://www.urban.org/toolkit/fivequestions/fortuny.cfm

Harris, C., Guenther, Z., Rosemarin, S., & Eriksson, G. (2009). *Gifted immigrants and refugees: The gold unmined.* Presentation at the 18th World Council for Gifted and Talented Children, Vancouver, Canada.

Harris, B., Rapp, K., Martinez, R., & Plucker, J. (2007). Identifying English language learners for gifted and talented programs: Current practices and recommendations for improvement. *Roeper Review, 29,* 26–29.

Hughes, C. E. (2011). Twice-exceptional children: Twice the challenges, twice the joys. In J. A. Castellano & A. D. Frazier (Eds.), *Special populations in gifted education: Understanding our most able students from diverse backgrounds* (pp. 153–174). Waco, TX: Prufrock Press.

Humes, K., Jones, N., & Ramirez, R. (2011). *2010 Census briefs: Overview of race and Hispanic origin: 2010.* C2010BR-02. Retrieved from http://www.census.gov/prod/cen2010/briefs/c2010br-02.pdf

Kitano, M. K., & Pedersen, K. S. (2002). Action research and practical inquiry teaching gifted English learners. *Journal for the Education of the Gifted, 26,* 132–147.

Kochlar, R., Fry, R., & Taylor, P. (2011). *Wealth gaps rise to record highs between Blacks, Whites, Hispanics.* Retrieved from http://www.pewsocialtrends.org/2011/07/26/wealth-gaps-rise-to-record-highs-between-whites-blacks-hispanics/

Krogstead, J. M. (2014, July 8). *A view of the future through Kindergarten demographics.* Pew Research Hispanic Trends Project. Retrieved from http://www.pewresearch.org/fact-tank/2014/07/08/a-view-of-the-future-through-kindergarten-demographics/

Krugman, V. K., & Iza, L. (2014). Building collaborative partnerships in schools and communities. In M. S. Matthews & J. A. Castellano

(Eds.), *Talent development for English language learners: Identifying and developing potential* (pp. 125–165). Waco, TX: Prufrock Press.

Lara-Alecio, R., & Irby, B. (2000). The culturally and linguistically diverse gifted. In C. Reynolds (Ed.), *Encyclopedia of special education* (pp. 506–510). New York, NY: Wiley.

Latz, A. O., & Adams, C. M. (2011). Critical differentiation and the twice oppressed: Social class and giftedness. *Journal for the Education of the Gifted, 34,* 773–789.

Leeks, R., & Stonehill, R. (2008, February). *Serving recent immigrant students through school-community partnerships.* Retrieved from http://www.ldonline.org/article/Serving_Recent_Immigrant_Students_Through_School-Community_Partnerships?theme=print

Lindsey, R., Robins, K., & Terrell, R. (2003). *Cultural proficiency: A manual for school leaders* (2nd ed.). Thousand Oaks, CA: Corwin Press.

Maker, C. J., & Schiever, S. W. (Eds.). (1989). *Critical issues in gifted education: Defensible programs for cultural and ethnic minorities* (Vol. II). Austin, TX: Pro-Ed.

Marland, S. P., Jr. (1972). *Education of the gifted and talented: Report to the Congress of the United States by the U.S. Commissioner of Education and background papers submitted to the U.S. Office of Education,* 2 vols. Washington, DC: U.S. Government Printing Office. (Government Documents, Y4.L 11/2: G36)

Naglieri, J., & Ford, D. (2003). Addressing underrepresentation of gifted minority children using the Naglieri nonverbal ability test (NNAT). *Gifted Child Quarterly, 47,* 155–160.

Neumeister, K., Adams, C., Pierce, R., Cassady, J., & Dixon, F. (2007). Fourth-grade teachers' perceptions of giftedness: Implications for identifying and serving diverse gifted students. *Journal for the Education of the Gifted, 30,* 479–499.

Orozco, G. (2008). Understanding the culture of low-income immigrant Latino parents: Key to involvement. *The School Community Journal, 18*(1), 21–37.

Orozco, G., & Thakore-Dunlap, U. (2010). *School counselors working with Latino children and families affected by deportation.* Retrieved from http://counselingoutfitters.com/vistas/vistas10/Article_80.pdf

Passel, J., & Cohen, D. (2009, April). *A portrait of unauthorized immigrants in the United States*. Pew Hispanic Center. Retrieved from http://www.pewhispanic.org/2009/04/14/a-portrait-of-unauthorized-immigrants-in-the-united-states/

Pereira, N., & Gentry, M. (2013). A qualitative inquiry into the experiences of high-potential Hispanic English language learners in Midwestern schools. *Journal of Advanced Academics, 24,* 164–194.

Peterson, J. (2006). Addressing counseling needs of gifted students. *Professional School Counseling, 10*(1), 43–51.

Renzulli, J. (1977). The enrichment triad model: A plan for developing defensible programs for the gifted. *Gifted Child Quarterly, 21,* 227–233.

Scott, M., Perou, R., Urbano, R., Hogan, A., & Gold, S. (1992). The identification of giftedness: A comparison of White, Hispanic and Black families. *Gifted Child Quarterly, 36,* 131–139.

U.S. Department of Education, Office of Educational Research. (1994). *National excellence: A case for developing America's talent*. Washington, DC: U.S. Government Printing Office.

VanTassel-Baska, J., & Johnsen, S. K. (2007). Teacher education standards for the field of gifted education: A vision of coherence for personnel preparation in the 21st century. *Gifted Child Quarterly, 51,* 182–205.

Van Velsor, P., & Orozco, G. (2007). Involving low income parents in the schools: Communitycentric strategies for school counselors. *Professional School Counseling Journal, 11*(1), 17–24.

Young, A. L. (2010, September). Developing teacher candidates' knowledge, skills and dispositions to teach diverse students (Report). *Journal of Instructional Psychology, 37,* 142–153.

CHAPTER 4

Gifted English Language Learners

The lack of attention to the identification of gifted English language learner (ELL) populations presents a significant weakness in gifted education research. With the rapid increase of diverse student populations across the nation, the underidentification and underrepresentation of English language learners in gifted education programs is a persistent problem that demands close examination (Harris, Rapp, Martinez, & Plucker, 2007; Matthews & Castellano, 2014; VanTassel-Baska & Stambaugh, 2007). Data collected and reported by the U.S. Department of Education Office for Civil Rights Data Collection (CRDC) on the percentages of Black, Hispanic, and White students in public schools and gifted education nationally, show that for all student groups for 2004, 2006, and 2012, every year, African American and Hispanic students are clearly and problematically underrepresented (Ford, 2013). Furthermore, these federal statistics reveal that hundreds of thousands of students in our public schools during 2009 were English language learners and the percentage/number is rising significantly. According to Castellano (2011), educational and instructional leaders in gifted education have a responsibility to promote equity and opportunity for gifted students of diverse backgrounds who have been historically underrepresented and underserved.

Despite the increased awareness for school districts and schools to identify and provide gifted programs to students within this subgroup equitably and defensively, many ELL students are not receiving the edu-

DOI: 10.4324/9781003235767-4

cational services necessary to develop their talents (Castellano & Díaz, 2002). The lack of an agreed upon definition or identification procedure is a frequently cited barrier to identifying, placing, and providing appropriate services to gifted culturally, linguistically, and/or ethnically diverse (CLED) students (Brulles, Castellano, & Laing, 2011; Cohen, 1990; Harris et al., 2007). Appropriate gifted identification practices and procedures are important because equitable placement of students in gifted programs helps ensure fair access to services, programs, and resources to all students.

CHARACTERISTICS OF GIFTED ENGLISH LANGUAGE LEARNERS

As the population of English language learners continues to grow, educators need to recognize that not all students will display their gifts through academic achievement and assessments. Furthermore, it is important to acknowledge diverse attributes, perspectives, and values of ELL students and how these can contribute to a broader concept of giftedness. Gifted ELL students have the same general abilities as many gifted students, yet because of cultural differences or lack of early experiences, they may not display the typical characteristics of intellectually gifted students that are often considered by teachers when making referrals to gifted education programs. The challenge is that educators of gifted and talented English language learners must be aware that students display their potential within the cultural context of learning a second language. It is this awareness that will assist educators in identifying the abilities and potential of English language learners.

The Iowa Department of Education, in collaboration with the Belin and Blank International Center for Gifted Education and Talent Development (2008), published a manual titled *Identifying Gifted and Talented English Language Learners in K–12*. The authors noted that this population of students may exhibit varying degrees of the following characteristics:

- acquires a second language rapidly,
- shows high ability in mathematics,

- displays a mature sense of diverse cultures and languages,
- code switches easily (thinks in both languages),
- demonstrates an advanced awareness of American expressions,
- translates at an advanced level (oral), and
- navigates appropriate behaviors successfully within both cultures.

These characteristics stemmed from their earlier work called Project GOTCHA (Galaxies of Thinking and Creative Heights of Achievement), a Title VII, Academic Excellence program, under the Office of Bilingual Education and Language Minority Affairs, U.S. Department of Education. The program identifies and serves gifted, creative, and talented limited English proficient (LEP) students in grades 1–8. According to Project GOTCHA, gifted and talented English language learners demonstrate the following characteristics in three domains: school-based, culture-based, and language-based:

SCHOOL-BASED DOMAIN:

- Are able to read in their native language two grade levels above their current grade.
- Show high ability in mathematics.
- Are advanced in creative domains (fluency, elaboration, originality, and flexibility).
- Are leaders in multiple settings (playground, home, clubs, etc.).

CULTURE-BASED DOMAIN:

- Balance behaviors expected in both the heritage and the new culture.
- Are willing to share their heritage culture.
- Show pride in their culture and ethnic background.
- Demonstrate a global sense of community and respect for cultural differences.

LANGUAGE-BASED DOMAIN:

- Demonstrate language proficiency levels that are above non-gifted students who are also English language learners.

- Learn multiple languages at an accelerated pace.
- Show the ability to code switch.
- Want to teach others words from their heritage language.
- Are willing to translate for others.
- Have superior knowledge of phrases and heritage dialects along with the ability to translate meanings in English.
- Have a grasp on jokes related to cultural differences.

They caution that that there is little research to support that such lists are reliable and valid ways of identifying gifted and talented ELL students, yet these observations can be a valuable supplement to standardized test scores in moving toward a more comprehensive identification process for selecting high potential English language learners for gifted and talented programming (Iowa Department of Education & Belin-Blank Center, 2008). ELL students' giftedness may manifest itself in ways that emphasize the students' linguistic, ethnic, and cultural backgrounds (Harris et al., 2007). When teachers are trained to recognize the characteristics of gifted ELLs, they are more likely to identify the students' ability or potential.

Identifying students for gifted programming typically begins at the classroom level and this identification informs curricular and instructional decisions for the student. Teachers' perceptions of the academic abilities of their students will greatly influence their instructional strategies and interactions with these students. Thus, identification procedures should concentrate on a broader conception of giftedness that includes nontraditional approaches that consider culture. Different cultures stress specific academic and intellectual abilities and talents; therefore, the ways that ELL students express giftedness and intellect are directly related to their cultural values. Traditional indicators of academic success skills may not necessarily match indicators of success for students of diverse cultures. Consequently, educators may overlook students who demonstrate culturally relevant gifts and talents that are not recognized or appreciated by the majority culture.

Brulles et al. (2011) acknowledged that in order to change how giftedness is viewed in students of different cultures, it is necessary to develop teachers' ability to recognize and capitalize on how these students demonstrate their talents and strengths. Identifying and assessing ELLs for gifted education programs must be an inclusive dynamic process that looks at these students holistically by assessing their potential strengths through multiple dimensions. Adapted from the works of Aguirre and Hernandez (1999) and Winebrenner and Brulles (2008), Brulles et al. (2011) added these additional characteristics:

- has a strong desire to learn in English and his or her heritage language;
- sees relationships and make connections;
- demonstrates exceptional talent in areas valued by his or her culture;
- assumes leadership roles with other students from same culture;
- carries responsibilities well; and
- demonstrates a richness in imaginary and formal language.

OBSTACLES TO IDENTIFYING AND ASSESSING GIFTED ENGLISH LANGUAGE LEARNERS

Despite increased awareness of the need to identify more ELL students for gifted programs and services, this population remains underrepresented in gifted and talented programs. The lack of explicit identification policies regarding proper and equitable identification of gifted students from underrepresented groups is a barrier to valid and reliable identification procedures. Matthews (2014) noted that grades are not as "strong of a predictor" of academic achievement for ELL students "because a still-developing English proficiency may artificially depress grades" (pp. 6–7). Harris, Plucker, Rapp, and Martinez (2009) cited additional barriers to effective practices for identifying ELL students as gifted and talented, including (a) low teacher expectations of minority students; (b) negative reactions by school personnel towards non-English-speaking students; (c) biases in standardized testing; and (d) the noninclusion or lack of cultural relevancy of the definition of giftedness. Harris et al. (2009) further suggested that one of the most underacknowledged components of the gifted and talented identification process involves educating parents and guardians about the gifted services available at the school. They suggested that schools need to assume responsibility to research and learn about their students' cultures because different cultures stress specific academic and intellectual abilities and talents. Thus, not only do language issues factor into identifying a student, but limited knowledge and parental awareness of the U.S. educational system also needs to be evaluated.

TEACHER ISSUES

Teachers' lack of knowledge and understanding of cultural, linguistic, and cognitive skills of ELL students is an obstacle to identification. Harris et al. (2009) stated that teachers are more likely to nominate students who exhibit characteristics that are traditionally recognized as advanced by mainstream culture; however, these qualities may not be advantageous or considered expressions of giftedness in other cultures. Often, due to the inherent cultural and language barriers between English language learners and U.S. schools, ELL students have fewer opportunities compared to their native English-speaking peers to be noticed by teachers for behaviors traditionally characteristic of gifted and talent students in the U.S. (Aguirre, 2003). Aptitudes and characteristics of talent potential are culturally defined and embedded, so when identifying gifted and talented students who have limited English proficiency, educators must do so within the context of the student's cultural and linguistic background. It is also important to understand, for example, that behaviors signaling giftedness in one culture may signal disrespect or hold some other negative connotation in another.

Although educators may assume an awareness of their own biases, they may have stereotypes and prejudices that devalue other cultures. Because less acculturated students in U.S. school settings may be perceived as "less bright" than more acculturated students, obtaining acculturation scale results can be valuable in helping prevent educators from inadvertently discriminating against certain groups of students (Iowa Department of Education & Belin-Blank Center, 2008). Even differences in English language learner dialects have been found to influence initial administrator and teacher judgments. Such judgments are critically important because they can influence how administrators and teachers view an English language learner's potential giftedness. If an educator stereotypes a certain culture as not valuing education, he or she is not as likely to view a student from that culture as bright. Research findings support that the limited inclusion of English language learners in gifted and talented programs is sometimes based on discriminatory attitudes (Harris et al., 2007; Harris et al., 2009; Iowa Department of Education & Belin-Blank Center, 2008; Lewis-Moreno, 2007). This attitude also may lead to fears that by admitting a student from that culture into the gifted and talented program, its quality will be watered-down or diminished.

ASSESSMENT ISSUES

Linguistically diverse students, referred for testing by their teachers, rarely qualify due to the overreliance on standardized tests administered in English (Castellano & Díaz, 2002). Heavy reliance on standardized tests results in diverse groups of students being unequally represented, with greater concentrations in special education classes and fewer concentrations in gifted and talented and advanced instructional programs. Many achievement and ability measures assume a certain kind of language socialization, and students who lack this socialization are, by definition, disadvantaged. Selecting tests that reduce cultural and linguistic bias is not an easy task, and it is questionable whether any test is truly "culture free" but tests can be culture reduced and thus increase in fairness (Ford, 2013). Instruments that can detect giftedness and talent in English language learners are sorely lacking, and inadequate assessment procedures continue to contribute to the underrepresentation of English language learners in gifted and talented programs.

BEST PRACTICES FOR IDENTIFYING GIFTED ENGLISH LANGUAGE LEARNERS

The literature suggests that there are multiple aspects of gifted programming that must be modified in order to succeed in identifying and successfully providing services to students not traditionally included in gifted programs (Cohen, 1990; Iowa Department of Education & Belin-Blank Center, 2008; Smutny & Danley, 2012). Educators should understand that the conceptualization of giftedness, and thus the services provided, are culturally manifested in each student's family and country of origin. Greater understanding and awareness of cultural differences and similarities will be needed to promote effective gifted education programs in the United States (Matthews & Castellano, 2014).

Matthews and Castellano (2014) also noted that the needs of gifted ELLs and highly able (potentially gifted) ELLs are met differently than typical English speaking students' needs are, and highly able ELLs have unique needs that can be addressed by combining gifted and ESL support services in a collaborative relationship with a classroom teacher. It has been discussed that giftedness in English language learners will manifest itself in ways that emphasize students' linguistic, ethnic, and cultural backgrounds. Therefore, assessment and referral practices should intend to be more inclusive of culturally-based characteristics of giftedness in order to reduce cultural and linguistic bias.

Identification and assessment of gifted ELL students can be complex because it involves students who are gifted and from a language or cultural background different from that of middle-class, native-English speaking children. The challenge often lies in determining what assessment tools to use and recognizing that any test written in English is not necessarily a true indicator of ability, but also a reflection of the student's current exposure to the English language. When an English language learner takes a test of academic content in English, he or she has a dual challenge: First, the student must understand the language and then respond to the content. The end result is that the student's lack of English skills will likely affect his or her test performance. Considering a student's level of English proficiency when making decisions about placement in gifted programming is not meant to be used as an exclusionary tool, but instead should be used to provide insight to the educational profile and complement other information provided about the student. Therefore, how the information is used from multiple sources is just as important as what information is used.

MULTIPLE MEASURES

As with other ethnically diverse groups, such as African American students, there are calls for the use of multiple criteria for identification as well as responsiveness to cultural factors and English language proficiency (Harris et al., 2007). Many researchers and practitioners recommend multiple assessment measures/data points to give ELL students several opportunities to demonstrate their skills and performance potential (Iowa Department of Education & Belin-Blank Center, 2008; Johnsen, 2011). They suggest that when evaluating any child for gifted programming, practitioners need to look at the whole child: the cognitive, affective, and psychomotor/behavioral domains. They propose that educators use the domains to document a child's unique abilities, because all three domains are interrelated. Keeping in mind the essential relationship among these three facets of a student's potential will assist in identifying giftedness even when a student is not fluent in English. Educators should take all possible steps to maximize a student's ability to express knowledge of content while minimizing the need to rely on English to express these ideas. At the same time, remember that, for many English language learners, their culture and experiences are very different from those of the English speakers who design and excel on assessment and ability tests. Educators are urged to use the three-domain model as a guide to describe and document academic potential and to construct a reliable and valid gifted English language learner profile.

COGNITIVE ASSESSMENTS

A score on a verbal or nonverbal test of ability has traditionally been the most common criterion for identification and placement of students in gifted and talented programs (Harris et al., 2007). Multiple issues should be considered when using cognitive ability measures to identify gifted and talented ELL students and other CLED students, such as whether the assessment accurately measures the intended construct and not additional extraneous factors. In a study comparing the validity of three nonverbal tests, the Raven's Standard Progressive Matrices (Raven), the Naglieri Nonverbal Ability Test (NNAT), and Form 6 of the Cognitive Abilities Test (CogAT) for the purpose of identifying academically gifted elementary English language learners, authors found that none of the nonverbal tests predicted achievement for ELL students very well (Lohman, Korb, & Lakin, 2008). ELL children in this study scored 8 to 10 points lower than non-ELL children on the three nonverbal tests. The study also showed that practitioners cannot assume that national norms on the tests are of comparable quality. Lohman, Korb, and Lakin (2008) suggested that when using national norms, both the Raven and NNAT will substantially overestimate the number of high-scoring children.

A possible alternative to using English language standardized tests and norms is to assess ELL students in their native language or compare ELL students' scores with other students in the district of the same age group with similar language and acculturation experiences (Iowa Department of Education & Belin-Blank Center, 2008). However, to ensure validity, the norms must be appropriate for the individual student based on his or her country of origin and linguistic heritage (Harris et al., 2007). One recommendation from Lohman et al. (2008) is to use local norms instead of national norms to evaluate giftedness and determine eligibility. For example, while an English language learner's score on the Verbal Reasoning subtest of the Cognitive Abilities Tests (CogAT) may not be outstanding when compared to an English speaker's Verbal Reasoning score, it may be unusually high compared to other English language learners in the school district and should be regarded as evidence of talent. Without considering local norms, the sole reliance on standardized tests, including tests of cognitive ability, to identify gifted students is widely considered inappropriate for ethnic and linguistic minorities, and has been cited as a root cause of underrepresentation.

In addressing the use of nonverbal assessments, Iowa Department of Education and the Belin-Blank Center (2008) stated that nonverbal assessments, by definition, do not rely on language, so some researchers suggest that these tests provide a more equitable method of identifying gifted/talented students from historically underrepresented populations. However, the user needs to consider if the directions and responses are also not language-based as well as the items. Their suitability for English language learners and bilingual students depends on the assessment not having elaborate verbal directions written in English.

Although nonverbal intelligence tests can be used to identify non-English speakers, it is important to remember the limitations of these measures (Worrell, 2013) and the drawbacks of using a single score (Worrell, 2009). The use of nonverbal assessments in isolation may even be more likely to exclude a gifted/talented learner who excels in other areas that have greater bearing on school success. For these reasons, screening for giftedness with nonverbal tests should be used as only one measure in a set of assessments to identify English language learners. One proposed solution is to assess students in all three symbol systems of language: verbal reasoning, nonverbal/spatial reasoning, and quantitative reasoning, and then pay attention to the highest scores within each ethnic and/or ELL group (Iowa Department of Education & Belin-Blank Center, 2008).

ELL students who have been in a U.S. school for one year need to have not only a high score on nonverbal tests but also would need to demonstrate upper level accomplishment in the particular subject area (such as math or reading) in which they will be placed in gifted programming. In addition, they would have to have a high score in comparison to other ELL students who had been in a U.S. school for the same length of time (Iowa Department of Education & Belin-Blank Center, 2008). In this sense, the use of nonverbal assessments (e.g., Comprehensive Test of Nonverbal Intelligence [CTONI], Universal Nonverbal Intelligence Test [UNIT], Test of Nonverbal Intelligence, Fourth Edition [TONI-4]) adds to the identification or admission decision.

Although there are no universally accepted procedures for identifying gifted and talented ELL students, best practices in psychological assessment emphasize authentic and dynamic methods and procedures (Castellano & Díaz, 2002). With dynamic-based or performance-based assessments, students are initially tested on material they do not know, receive an intervention, and then are retested to see what improvements resulted from the intervention. In this sense, what is being tested is their ability to use cognitive strategies to master new materials.

The use of multiple criteria and nontraditional assessments along with the use of intelligence tests and measures of achievement is a gifted education program standard for the identification of giftedness (Johnsen, 2012), especially with nonmajority and ELL populations (Harris et al., 2007). Furthermore, authentic and dynamic procedures for identifying gifted and talented ELL students include but are not limited to classroom observations, checklists and rating scales, portfolio evaluations, nominations, teacher nominations, problem-solving based assessments, interviews with parents and communities, self-identification, and alternative testing.

A Florida Department of Education (1998) technical assistance paper, intended to assist school districts in identifying Limited English Proficient students for eligibility in gifted programs, recommends the following techniques or tools for screening potentially gifted ELL students:

- parent interview to elicit evidence of behaviors in the home and community setting;
- academic assessment, irrespective of English proficiency;
- academic skills not dependent on English language (e.g., mathematics calculations, problem solving using visual-spatial reasoning);
- nonverbal cognitive screening and identification tests;
- curriculum-based assessment (if used with accommodations for native language);
- student interviews;
- review of prior school records and performance including scores on test in native language;
- work samples in native language and in English;
- observations of student by school personnel, especially by those who are proficient in the student's native language;
- interviews with teachers with special consideration of ELL teachers, bilingual paraprofessionals, and other personnel who work with the student;
- interviews with appropriate people with knowledge of the student/family (clergy, former teachers, pediatrician, etc.); and

- test-educate-test paradigms to assess the modifiability of a student's cognitive processes.

A major shortcoming continues to be the major focus on testing—not culture. Ford (2013) urged educators to always be mindful of equitable or multicultural testing and assessment principles, and for all decision makers and educators to adopt and adhere to culturally responsive and fair assessment principles when providing services to students who differ from the norming sample and who are frequently negatively impacted by tests (i.e., linguistically, economically, racially, and culturally different students).

CONCLUSION

For many people, the concept of "giftedness" equates to high academic achievement. For English language learners who are not yet fluent in English, this is an inequitable standard. It excludes English language learners and other CLED children who do not do well on academic assessments but who have elevated general abilities as measured by nonverbal assessments of ability. Formal communication and ongoing professional development opportunities with classroom teachers, ELL staff, and gifted and talented program teachers are central to the success of identifying and serving ELL students in gifted and talented programs. This facilitates ongoing collaboration, provides a more holistic student profile and aids identification of all potentially gifted ELL students. Krugman and Iza (2014) suggested that collaborative partnerships can help address the needs of highly able ELLs, especially when gifted programs work collaboratively with ESL programs to "build stronger instructional relationships and processes for addressing the language and cultural issues of the highly able ELLs" (p. 127).

Developing appropriate identification procedures is important, but the system policies and school administration must also promote, emphasize, and monitor these procedures. In addition to promoting equity and access, an emphasis on an authentic identification protocol carried out by qualified personnel and best practices in identification of gifted and talented ELL students must become nonnegotiable.

REFERENCES

Aguirre, N. (2003). ESL students in gifted education. In J. A. Castellano (Ed.), *Special populations in gifted education: Working with diverse gifted learners* (pp. 17–27). Boston, MA: Allyn & Bacon.

Aguirre, N., & Hernandez, N. (1999). *Characteristics of students who are linguistically and culturally diverse.* Baton Rouge, LA: Modern Language Services.

Brulles, D., Castellano, J. A., & Laing, P. (2011). Identifying and enfranchising gifted English language learners. In J. A. Castellano & A. D. Frazier (Ed.), *Special populations in gifted education: Understanding our most valuable students from diverse backgrounds* (pp. 305–313). Waco, TX: Prufrock Press.

Castellano, J. A. (2011). Hispanic students and gifted education: New outlooks, perspectives and paradigms. In J. A. Castellano & A. D. Frazier (Eds.), *Special populations in gifted education: Understanding our most valuable students from diverse backgrounds* (pp. 249–269). Waco, TX: Prufrock Press.

Castellano, J. A., & Díaz, E. (2002). *Reaching new horizons: Gifted and talented education for culturally and linguistically diverse students.* Boston, MA: Allyn & Bacon.

Cohen, L. (1990). *Meeting the needs of gifted and talented minority language students.* (ERIC Digest E480). ERIC Clearinghouse on Handicapped and Gifted Children. Reston, VA.

Florida Department of Education. (1998). *Assessing limited English proficient (LEP) students for eligibility for gifted programs.* Retrieved from http://www.fldoe.org/ese/pdf/tap99-6.pdf

Ford, D. Y. (2013). *Recruiting and retaining culturally different students in gifted education.* Waco, TX: Prufrock Press.

Harris, B., Plucker, J., Rapp, K., & Martinez, R. (2009). Identifying gifted and talented English language learners: A case study. *Journal for the Education of the Gifted, 32,* 368–393.

Harris, B., Rapp, K., Martinez, R., & Plucker, J. (2007). Identifying English language learners for gifted and talented programs: Current practices and recommendations for improvement. *Roeper Review, 29*(5), 26–29.

Iowa Department of Education, & The Connie Belin and Jacqueline N. Blank International Center for Gifted Education and Talent Development. (2008). *Identifying gifted and talented English language learners grades K–12*. Des Moines, IA: Authors.

Johnsen, S. K. (2011). *Identifying gifted students: A practical guide* (2nd ed.). Waco, TX: Prufrock Press.

Johnsen, S. K. (Ed.). (2012). *Using the NAGC Pre-K–Grade 12 gifted programming standards*. Waco, TX: Prufrock Press.

Krugman, V. K., & Iza, L. (2014). Building collaborative partnerships in schools and communities. In M. S. Matthews & J. A. Castellano (Eds.), *Talent development for English language learners: Identifying and developing potential* (pp. 125–165). Waco, TX: Prufrock Press.

Lohman, D., Korb, K., & Lakin, J. (2008). Identifying academically gifted English language learners using nonverbal tests: A comparison of the Raven, NNAT, and CogAT. *Gifted Child Quarterly, 52,* 275–296.

Lewis-Moreno, B. (2007). Shared responsibility: Achieving success with English-Language Learners. *Phi Delta Kappan, 88*(10), 772.

Matthews, M. S. (2014). Advanced academics, inclusive education, and English language learners. In M. S. Matthews & J. A. Castellano (Eds.), *Talent development for English language learners: Identifying and developing potential* (pp. 1–13). Waco, TX: Prufrock Press.

Matthews, M. S., & Castellano, J. A. (Eds.). (2014). *Talent development for English language learners: Identifying and developing potential.* Waco, TX: Prufrock Press.

Smutny, J. F., & Danley, G. (2012). Unmasking potential. *Principal Leadership, 12,* 53–57.

VanTassel-Baska, J., & Stambaugh, T. (2007). *Overlooked gems: A national perspective on low-income promising learners.* Washington, DC: National Association of Gifted Children.

Winebrenner, S., & Brulles, D. (2008). *The cluster grouping handbook: How to challenge gifted students and improve achievement for all.* Minneapolis, MN: Free Spirit.

Worrell, F. C. (2009). Myth 4: A single test score or indicator tells us all we need to know about giftedness. *Gifted Child Quarterly, 53,* 242–244.

Worrell, F. C. (2013). Identifying gifted learners: Nonverbal assessment. In C. M. Callahan & H. Hertberg-Davis (Eds.), *Fundamentals of gifted education: Considering multiple perspectives* (pp. 135–147). New York, NY: Routledge.

CHAPTER 5

Twice-Exceptional Students

Twice-exceptional students are defined as students with gifts and talents who also have one or more disabilities (NAGC, 2009). They "exhibit remarkable strength in some areas and disabling weaknesses in others" (Weinfeld, Barnes-Robinson, Jeweler, & Shevitz, 2002, p. 226). Twice-exceptional students have "extraordinary strengths and each one of them has extraordinary challenges . . . [they] are gifted yet also have a disability that impacts their ability to fully develop in all areas" (Hughes, 2011, p. 154). Additionally, the strengths and weakness these students possess may mask each other (Silverman, 1993). Estimates suggest there are approximately 300,000 twice-exceptional students in United States' schools, but no federal agency collects prevalence data for this population (Baum & Owen, 2004; NAGC, 2009). Twice-exceptional students come in a variety of shapes, sizes, and abilities; no two twice-exceptional students are precisely alike, as there are many ways for them to demonstrate gifted potential and many different ways for their disability(ies) to be manifested. Due to their uniqueness and paradoxical characteristics, twice-exceptional students are often an enigma to both their parents and teachers (Hughes, 2011; Roberts & Jolly, 2012) as well as to the other students around them.

 DOI: 10.4324/9781003235767-5

CHARACTERISTICS OF TWICE-EXCEPTIONAL LEARNERS

Much of the research literature on this population focuses on gifted students with specific learning disabilities (SLD), Attention Deficit/Hyperactivity Disorder (ADHD), and autism spectrum disorders such as Asperger's syndrome (Foley Nicpon, Allmon, Sieck, & Stinson, 2011) or high-functioning autism (Silverman, Kenworthy, & Weinfeld, 2014). According to Baum, Cooper, and Neu (2001), a typical twice-exceptional learner profile includes, "a propensity for advanced-level content, a desire to create original products, a facility with and enjoyment of abstract concepts, nonlinear learning styles, task commitment in areas of talent and interest, an identification with others of similar talents and interests, and a heightened sensitivity to failure or injustice" (p. 481), as well as simultaneously weaker development in the following areas: academic achievement, organization, attention, social skills, and self-efficacy and self-esteem. These paradoxical characteristics can impact the child's academic performance as well as his or her social-emotional skill development and/or functioning (Hughes, 2011).

COMMON STRENGTHS

Twice-exceptional learners have gifts and talents similar to those of gifted students without disabilities while also presenting weaknesses due to the impact of their disability(ies); these are described in Table 5.1. Trail (2011) highlighted the following as common strengths: superior vocabulary, highly creative, resourceful, curious, imaginative, questioning, problem-solving ability, sophisticated sense of humor, wide range of interests, advanced ideas and opinions, and special talent or consuming interest. Although every student is unique, even amongst twice-exceptional students, empirical studies consistently show advanced verbal ability to be a strength for most twice-exceptional students (Foley Nicpon et al., 2011). Teachers and parents will often notice students with this strength right away, as this gift can be evident just by speaking with the twice-exceptional student. In our experience, these students often have extensive background knowledge and use advanced vocabulary and com-

TABLE 5.1
COMPARISON OF CHARACTERISTICS OF GIFTED
STUDENTS WITH OR WITHOUT DISABILITIES

Characteristics of Gifted Students Without Disabilities	Characteristics of Gifted Students With Disabilities
Ability to learn basic skills quickly and easily and retain information with less repetition	Often struggle to learn basic skills due to cognitive processing difficulties; need to learn compensatory strategies in order to acquire basic skills and information
High verbal ability	High verbal ability, but extreme difficulty in written language area; may use language in inappropriate ways and at inappropriate times
Early reading ability	Frequently have reading problems due to cognitive processing deficits
Keen powers of observation	Strong observation skills, but often have deficits in memory skills
Strong critical thinking, problem-solving, and decision-making skills	Excel in solving real-world problems; outstanding critical thinking and decision-making skills; often independently develop compensatory skills
Long attention span—persistent, intense concentration	Frequently have attention deficit problems, but may concentrate for long periods in areas of interest
Questioning attitude	Strong questioning attitudes; may appear disrespectful when questioning information, facts, etc. presented by teacher
Creative in the generation of thoughts, ideas, actions; innovative	Unusual imagination; frequently generate original and, at times, rather bizarre ideas; extremely divergent in thought; may appear to daydream when generating ideas
Take risks	Often unwilling to take risks with regard to academics; take risks in nonschool areas without consideration of consequences
Unusual, often highly developed sense of humor	Humor may be used to divert attention from school failure; may use humor to make fun of peers or to avoid trouble
May mature faster at different rates than age peers	Sometimes appears immature because they may use anger, crying, withdrawal, etc. to express feelings and to deal with difficulties
Sense of independence	Require frequent teacher support and feedback in deficit areas; highly independent in other areas; often appear to be extremely stubborn and inflexible

TABLE 5.1, CONTINUED

Characteristics of Gifted Students Without Disabilities	Characteristics of Gifted Students With Disabilities
Sensitive	Sensitive regarding disability area(s); highly critical of self and others including teachers; can express concern about the feelings of others even while engaging in antisocial behavior
May not be accepted by other children and may feel isolated	May not be accepted by other children and may feel isolated; may be perceived as loners, because they do not fit typical model for either a gifted or a learning disabled student; sometimes have difficulty being accepted by peers due to poor social skills
Exhibit leadership ability	Exhibit leadership ability; often leader among the more nontraditional students; demonstrate strong streetwise behavior; the disability may interfere with ability to exercise leadership skills
Wide range of interests	Wide range of interests, but are handicapped in pursuing them due to process/learning problems
Very focused interests (i.e., a passion about certain topics to the exclusion of others)	Very focused interests (i.e., a passion about a certain topic to the exclusion of others) often not related to school subjects

Note. From *Smart Kids With Learning Difficulties: Overcoming Obstacles and Realizing Potential* (2nd ed., pp. 26–27) by R. Weinfeld, L. Barnes-Robinson, S. Jeweler, and B. R. Shevitz, 2014, New York, NY: Taylor & Francis. Copyright 2014 Taylor & Francis. Reprinted with permission.

plex language. They often understand the nuances of figurative language, humor, and multiple meanings. They may be the only student to laugh at the teacher's jokes or to make classroom contributions that other students do not understand. Additionally, twice-exceptional students often show literal and inferential comprehension of complex text (some students may need to have the text read to them, if there is a reading deficit). Students with verbal strengths may excel in oral presentations, classroom discussions, and debates.

Some twice-exceptional students possess advanced visual-spatial reasoning ability and may be thought of as spatial learners (Mann, 2006; Silverman, 2002). These students are able to make sense of the world around them and problem-solve through the use of images, visualization, and interacting with concepts with their eyes and bodies. They think in pictures versus in words and they see how things connect and are interrelated. Hence, spatial learners often shine in math, science, and art classes (Silverman, 2002).

Twice-exceptional students are generally very curious and love to learn (unless this love of learning has been squelched). Baum et al. (2001) concluded that these children are able to demonstrate gifted intellectual ability and creativity, given appropriate supports. We have found that twice-exceptional students are extremely curious and creative individuals. They ask a lot of questions as they seek to broaden their knowledge and understand how concepts and ideas relate to one another. They enjoy developing new ideas, inventing new things, solving novel problems, and creating original products. Although writing is generally difficult for these students, many of these students enjoy creating stories or poems. These students love a challenge and would often prefer to work on a "hard" assignment versus what one might consider an "easy" task. Many of these students have the innate ability to think critically by forming judgments and supporting their conclusions with evidence. Mathematical thinking and reasoning is often an area of strength for twice-exceptional students.

COMMON WEAKNESSES

Twice-exceptional students have one or more disabilities that interfere with their ability to perform at a level commensurate with their abilities. The disability can interfere with learning in different ways depending on the nature of the disability and the manifestation within the individual student. Often, students with specific learning disabilities (SLD) have deficits in basic academic skills such as decoding, reading fluency, spelling, handwriting, math calculation, and written expression. Students with ADHD may possess average to above-average academic skills but have difficulty demonstrating their skills consistently due to difficulties with organization, executive functioning, concentration, and focus. Students with Asperger's syndrome (now labeled under high-functioning autism with the 2013 edition of the *Diagnostic and Statistical Manual of Mental Disorders* [APA, 2013]) often struggle with social interactions, written expression, organization, and appropriate classroom behavior (Foley Nicpon et al., 2011, Silverman et al., 2014).

Despite the differences that exist between different populations of twice-exceptional students, there are common weaknesses that educators and parents can look for as they begin to suspect that a student with gifts and talents may also have a disability.

Many twice-exceptional students with specific learning disabilities struggle with writing, particularly when you compare their academic achievement in this area to their verbal gifts (Assouline, Foley Nicpon, & Whiteman, 2010). Putting their ideas on paper in writing can be a Herculean task for these students. If there are executive functioning difficulties, twice-exceptional students may struggle with developing their ideas fully, selecting a topic from all of the ideas swimming around in their head, organizing their ideas, deciding how to begin and sequence their writing, and managing time throughout the writing process. Additionally, many twice-exceptional students with writing disabilities have difficulty spelling, holding the words in their heads as they write (poor working memory), and handwriting and letter formation.

Assouline et al. (2010) found that reading skill levels of twice-exceptional students varied widely. For students with a reading disability, decoding, sight word recognition, and fluency are often the areas most impacted. These students often have excellent listening comprehension due to their strong verbal ability, but struggle to access text and to gain meaning from words on the page. Assouline et al. (2010) also determined that while the math knowledge of assessed twice-exceptional students was typically at or above grade level, their ability to solve simple math computation problems was lower. This poor math fluency shows in the classroom when these students struggle to acquire and develop automaticity with basic math facts and computation. Organization is also a challenge for many of these students and they may have difficulty organizing their writing or taking organized notes (Baum et al., 2001; Weinfeld et al., 2014). In our experience, twice-exceptional students often have difficulty initiating and completing tasks independently. They struggle to follow multistep directions or to take a long-term assignment and break it down into the component parts. Incomplete assignments and late work are common problems for these students. Their binders, desks, cubbies, and lockers may be stuffed with old, crumpled papers and odds and ends.

Many twice-exceptional students also have attention issues (either due to ADHD or due to boredom) that make it hard for them to concentrate and to sustain motivation and effort, particularly during non-preferred tasks (Baum et al., 2001). These students may be physically overactive and impulsive (calling-out, moving about the classroom, fidgeting) or distractible and inattentive (daydreaming, reading a book in their desks; Montgomery County Public Schools, 2007).

Many twice-exceptional students also face coexisting emotional and behavioral challenges such as depression and low self-esteem due to their school frustration and failure (Assouline, Foley Nicpon, & Huber, 2006; Foley Nicpon et al., 2011). The dichotomy of their strengths and weaknesses and the impact this has on their school performance makes them emotionally vulnerable, misunderstood, and unable to live up to the expectations placed upon them by parents, teachers, and themselves. Students on the autism spectrum (as well as other students with disabilities) may have difficulty with pragmatic language and have social skill deficits. Many students (regardless of label) have difficulty connecting with their same-age peers. They often get along well with adults and younger children but just don't have much in common with kids their own age. These students can be extremely hard on themselves and are vulnerable to feelings of sadness and worry related to their school performance (Shevitz, Stemple, Barnes-Robinson, & Jeweler, 2011). Barber and Mueller (2011) found that twice-exceptional adolescents rated themselves lower in areas of self-concept than did their "gifted only," "LD only," or unidentified counterparts. It is not easy to be gifted when you have a disability. Twice-exceptional students are keenly aware of their differences and what they often view as shortcomings. In our experience, they often feel as though they don't fit in with anyone as they may not know any other children who are smart and face learning difficulties like they do.

PULLING IT ALL TOGETHER

When each set of characteristics is viewed in isolation, the strengths described above are not uncommon, nor are the weaknesses, but finding the extreme strengths and significant weaknesses within one individual is not common, and it can be surprising. For example, a student may have a wealth of background knowledge and can engage in adult-like conversation about current events, but cannot read grade-level text. Or, a student may grasp mathematical concepts years above grade level, but cannot follow the morning routine independently and can't spell basic sight words. Thus, teachers must be trained to look for strengths and weaknesses that are seemingly contradictory, but actually confirm a suspicion that a student may be twice exceptional (Morrison & Rizza, 2007).

OBSTACLES TO IDENTIFYING TWICE-EXCEPTIONAL LEARNERS

Twice exceptionality is a fairly rare phenomenon, which means that many educators may not have the experience needed to recognize and identify these students (Foley Nicpon et al., 2011; Foley Nicpon, Assouline, & Colangelo, 2013; Hughes, 2011). It is commonly acknowledged that recognition and identification of twice-exceptional learners can be problematic, as it can be difficult for educators to imagine that a student could possess such a unique array of impressive strengths and perplexing weaknesses (Baum & Owen, 2004; Hughes, 2011; Morrison & Rizza, 2007) at the same time.

LACK OF AWARENESS

One major obstacle to identification of these students is lack of awareness (Hughes, 2011; Morrison & Rizza, 2007). The classroom teacher (or educational team) may see the strengths and weaknesses but not be aware that it is possible to be both gifted and have a disability. If classroom teachers are not aware of these students' characteristics, they won't be looking for students who fit the profile. Teachers must have the awareness and capacity to identify twice-exceptional students by receiving professional development about gifted students with disabilities' common strengths and weaknesses.

MASKED GIFTS

Another challenge to identification involves the concept of the "masking" of the gifts and/or the disability (Brody & Mills, 1997; Foley Nicpon et al., 2011, Weinfeld et al., 2014). The student's disability could affect his or her performance on assessments and in the classroom. Educators may see the student as gifted but unmotivated, or they may only see the disability. Or even worse, they may just view him or her as average. As a result, they may provide the child with either on-level, advanced, or remedial instruction, when in fact the student requires *both* challenging instruction and support.

AVERAGE EXPECTATIONS

Another obstacle to timely identification of these students may be the belief that meeting grade-level benchmarks or "average performance" is the end goal for all students. The focus in schools in recent years has been on getting students to achieve "proficiency" in the core academic areas of reading and math. It may take time for the gap between ability and achievement within a gifted student to widen enough for underachievement to be noted. Therefore, many of these students are not identified in the early years of elementary school when other students of their same age are still also learning basic skills. The signs of a potential learning problem may be evident (i.e., difficulty with letter/sound relationships, poor memory for spelling or math concepts), particularly in light of how smart a student appears to be, but these skill difficulties are developmentally appropriate and therefore, typically not considered to be red flags. Also, many of these students can compensate for their weaknesses with their strengths at this stage. It is often only when the student starts matriculating through the grades and the skill deficits remain that school teams become concerned. It is critical that school teams recognize average achievement or performance in a gifted student with superior cognitive ability as possible signs of a disability.

UNCHALLENGING CURRICULUM

Another issue impeding identification of these kids may be the curriculum itself. With a focus on the basics and less time thinking critically or engaging with science and social studies, students of today may have less of an opportunity to demonstrate their strengths and to have their gifts noticed. A classroom focusing on differentiation that allows students to study advanced concepts as they are ready, that is driven by critical and creative thinking tasks, and that utilizes multi-sensory instruction and multiple ways to show knowledge, is a classroom where students' gifts can shine through and be recognized. It is easy for the twice-exceptional student's strengths to go unrecognized in a traditional classroom where everyone studies the same thing at the same pace and where paper-and-pencil tasks are the rule of thumb.

INEFFECTIVE PROCESSES AND POLICIES

School policies and processes may also be inherent obstacles for twice-exceptional students. Many policies and processes are based on the premise that underachievement is the starting point for professional team problem solving around areas of concern. The twice-exceptional student may never be brought to the team's attention because the teacher has other students who are performing more poorly, because the student is meeting benchmarks with support, or because the student is making some incremental progress. School teams must begin to appreciate that average performance or failure to thrive for a gifted student is a sign of a possible disability. Significant underachievement for a gifted student means that educators have let the problem go on for far too long. Teams should consider interventions for students that address both their gifts and their learning challenges. If the student fails to make expected progress given the established interventions, formal evaluation for a suspected disability may be warranted.

RESPONSE TO INTERVENTION

EARLY INTERVENTIONS

Response to Intervention (RtI) is a process developed to provide early support and interventions to struggling learners, but its application can be extended to include problem-solving regarding children who are gifted (The Association for the Gifted, Council for Exceptional Children [CEC-TAG] & National Association for Gifted Children [NAGC], 2009) and students who are twice-exceptional (Council for Exceptional Children [CEC], 2007; CEC-TAG & NAGC, 2009; Pereles, Omdal, & Baldwin, 2009). A gifted student may require interventions to support his or her access to accelerated or enriched curriculum and instruction. A struggling student will require interventions to address his or her learning needs and to support his or her access to the general curriculum. In the case of a gifted student with potential disabilities, he or she will need interventions to address his or her gifts as well as his or her weaknesses (CEC-TAG & NAGC, 2009; Trail, 2011; Pereles et al., 2009). A system where interventions are provided to address strengths *and* weaknesses can meet the needs of twice-exceptional students. RtI may be a promising fit for problem solving regarding twice-exceptional learners, as a well-designed model can focus problem solving on both the gifts and the needs and eliminates the need to "wait to fail," which may avoid the development of social-emotional problems (Trail, 2011; Pereles et al., 2009).

IDENTIFICATION OF A SPECIFIC LEARNING DISABILITY

IDEA (2004) permits states to utilize RtI as the process for identifying students with a Specific Learning Disability. The National Association for Gifted Children (2009) highlighted potential problems with using RtI to identify gifted students with learning disabilities. One concern is that the general curriculum may not be a good match for a gifted student and so these students may not meet the threshold for failure within this context. Their performance may be viewed as adequate because they are underchallenged by the curriculum. This could result in the exact "wait to fail" scenario that RtI is attempting to prevent. Thus, all along the way with RtI, the strengths must be acknowledged and then ultimately, if a learning disability is suspected, a cognitive ability test should be included in the comprehensive evaluation (Assouline et al., 2010; NAGC, 2009; Pereles et al., 2009). That way, strengths and abilities can be considered for problem solving and identification of the disability, allowing fewer students to fall through the cracks by appearing average.

BEST PRACTICES FOR IDENTIFYING TWICE-EXCEPTIONAL LEARNERS

The suspected or identified disability may be a specific learning disability in reading, writing, or math; an autism spectrum disorder; ADHD; a vision or hearing impairment, or any number of other disabilities or impairments recognized by federal and state regulations. Criteria for eligibility is dependent upon federal law and regulations (IDEA, 2004), but identification processes for gifted and/or special education services can vary from state to state and district to district. In order to appropriately evaluate and identify twice-exceptional students, teams must have knowledge and experience with twice-exceptional students and must collect and consider data *from a variety of sources* carefully and intentionally (Shevitz et al., 2011).

COLLECTING DATA

When considering the possibility that a student is twice-exceptional, it is essential to collect formal and informal data from a variety of sources in order to identify the student's strengths as well as his or her weaknesses. In a formal evaluation, this would typically include measures of cognition and intelligence (IQ) as well as measures of academic achievement (Foley Nicpon et al., 2011). If there are concerns, a speech language evaluation or occupational therapy evaluation may be necessary. Depending on the disability, the evaluation may also include rating scales to determine the student's executive functioning, attention, social, and emotional levels. Informal and curriculum measures (e.g., informal reading inventories, math probes, multiple writing probes, classroom work samples) are equally important to consider, as this information can round out the formal data and help the team to better understand what the student can and can't do in the classroom. Observations of the student during routine classroom instruction can be incredibly informative, but it is important to remember that more than one observation may be needed to document both the strengths and weaknesses of the student. Therefore, the student should be formally observed in subjects where he or she shows strengths as well as in subjects where there are concerns. Teacher reports and anecdotal data from all classes/subjects should be considered as well. Considering input from multiple perspectives and stakeholders is essential for twice-exceptional students. The art or science teacher may have unique knowledge of a student's strengths or weaknesses, so it is recommended that input be solicited from all adults who interact with the student at school. Parental input is crucial because parents are often the first to see the gifts or the learning difficulties within their child. An informal interview with the student will often shed light on his or her strengths and weaknesses as well as how he or she is feeling about school. A twice-exceptional student who is failing to thrive will often have a depleted self-esteem and feel like a failure, even if he or she is meeting grade-level benchmarks. These students perceive the gaps between what they can do and what they can't do profoundly. They are often very sensitive and frustrated with their inability to perform up to their own expectations. Imagine if you had a brain that could think a mile a minute, but you were constantly being asked to show what you know by writing four words per minute. This frustration wears on these students over time, and educators can use the signs of strain as evidence that things are not working, especially when the data are "muddy" with highs, lows, and in-betweens, as often occurs.

CAREFUL DATA ANALYSIS

Once all of the data have been collected, it is important that the team analyze and interpret the data carefully to identify patterns of strengths and weaknesses. Otherwise, educators may wrongly conclude that the student is average, when he or she is in fact twice exceptional. Teams should review and consider individual data points such as subtest or clusters of scores as opposed to overrelying on broad or overall scores. For example, on a cognitive assessment, the team should notice a superior General Ability Index as opposed to focusing on an average full scale IQ (Foley Nicpon et al., 2011). As another example, teachers should notice the higher and lower grades that comprise the overall grade instead of focusing on an overall grade in the B or C range. When looking at reading inventory data, instead of saying the student is instructional at grade 4, educators might say that the student can decode words in isolation at second grade but can comprehend text read independently at grade 4 and can comprehend text read to him or her at grade 6. Instead of looking at the total scores on achievement tests, teachers should look at cluster scores or subtest scores. It is important to interpret the data carefully by drilling down and noticing patterns of strengths and weaknesses within and between the data sets. Many researchers recommend comparing the individual to themselves ("intraindividual") as opposed to others ("interindividual"; Foley Nicpon et al., 2011), because significant differences between strengths and weaknesses can then be noted.

It is also essential that teams compare the student's performance in the classroom to that of his or her gifted peers as opposed to arbitrary benchmarks or age/grade-level expectations. According to NAGC (2009), the assumption that the general classroom curriculum is a good match for a gifted student is wrong, and thus, the definition for failure for a child who is cognitively gifted cannot be based on adequate performance within this curriculum. Gifted students (whether or not a disability is suspected) should be provided with appropriate challenge and their performance and progress should be gauged within the context of this curriculum and in relation to their high-ability peers.

A national survey (Foley Nicpon et al., 2013) shed some light on familiarity and experience of educators (classroom teachers, gifted specialists, school psychologists, and special educators) as it relates to twice-exceptionality. The results were positive in that educators felt mostly familiar with the general concept and were fairly confident in their ability to make referrals for an evaluation of a disability for these students. However, surveyed educators said they had "passing" or "no" familiarity and "some" or "none" experience with the following groups of students at the following rates: 14.9%/39% familiarity/experience with gifted students with ADHD, 22.6%/50.5% familiarity/experience with gifted students with autism spectrum disorder, 18.3%/39.2% familiarity/experience with gifted students with emotional difficulties, and 20.6%/45.4% familiarity/experience with gifted students with learning disabilities. This suggests that approximately 1 in 4 or 5 evaluating team members have virtually no awareness of these students and many more may have little to no actual experience working with these students. Given this, and the level of knowledge and experience that is needed, it is recommended that each evaluation team include at least one member with knowledge of the characteristics and needs of twice-exceptional students (Shevitz et al., 2011).

MATCH SERVICES TO STRENGTHS AND NEEDS

Once identified, "services must match the needs [of the] twice-exceptional child" (Roberts & Jolly, 2012, p. 41). It is critical that students receive the following four components as part of their school program: (a) access to appropriately challenging instruction and gifted education opportunities, (b) instruction in their areas of weakness and disability, (c) instructional adaptations and accommodations, and (d) case management with social-emotional support and quality coordination of all of the parts of their program (Weinfeld et al., 2002). Inclusion of all four of these aspects of their programming is important because twice-exceptional students have tremendous potential that can either be squelched or unleashed. Without one or more of these best practices, these students often fail to thrive. They may get by in school, earning passing grades and attending on-level classes, while suffering from poor self-esteem and making only incremental progress. With the right supports, twice-exceptional students can excel academically, feel competent as learners, develop their talents, and reach their full potential.

Baum et al. (2001) described what these students need as a "dually-differentiated" curriculum to meet the talents and advanced learning needs of these students while simultaneously providing them with supports and compensatory strategies to address the learning weaknesses. These students flourish when provided with authentic learning experiences that allow them to access information in alternative ways and to problem solve and create products utilizing their strengths. The "dually-differentiated" curriculum allows for choice, self-direction, and freedom in the learning process, which empowers these students to succeed as learners.

Mann (2006) suggested that GT/LD students with spatial strengths should be offered choices, allowed to explore their interests, be afforded opportunities for experiential learning, and be provided with instruction that emphasizes conceptual understanding in a whole-to-part approach. Coleman (2005) established that for twice-exceptional students to succeed, it is critical to activate background knowledge, to build conceptual frameworks that emphasize the whole over parts, and to help students develop structures that promote an organized approach to learning. She emphasized the importance of maintaining highly complex lesson concepts/topics with scaffolding and support for the disability as opposed to reducing the level of complexity, an approach often taken with learning disabled students.

Despite the lack of empirical research regarding instructional techniques and interventions for twice-exceptional students (Foley Nicpon et al., 2011), the consensus among researchers and practitioners alike is that these students need an educational approach that addresses and focuses on their gifts and strengths while supporting and remediating the areas of weakness (Baum et al., 2001; Baum & Owen, 2004; Brody & Mills, 1997; Coleman, 2005; Foley Nicpon et al., 2011; Montgomery County Public Schools, 2004, 2007; Pereles et al., 2009; Shevitz et al., 2011; Trail, 2011; Weinfeld et al., 2014; Yssel, Prater, & Smith, 2010). In order to be done well, this requires a team approach whereby the special education teacher, the gifted teacher, the classroom teacher, the school counselor, and the parents work together to develop appropriate programming for these students (Yssel et al., 2010).

CONCLUSION

Once identified as gifted with a disability, twice-exceptional students are more likely to access accelerated and enriched instruction with the supports necessary for them to be successful. With access to gifted education opportunities, students can build upon their strengths, develop a positive self-concept, and nurture their passions and interests, both in and outside of the school building. The future can be bright for twice-exceptional students who are identified and served well in our schools, but we have to find them in order to serve them. This "child-find" process must be proactive as opposed to reactive, because these students often mask their gifts and/or disabilities in the early years. Educators need to universally screen for these students and train all teachers to recognize the common profiles of twice-exceptional students. It is crucial that school teams responsible for identifying twice-exceptional students be aware that data indicating strengths does not contradict or "rule out" the possibility of a disability. A student cannot be too smart to have a disability. The presence of gifts and a disability can result in average grades or average performance on districtwide assessments. Although the disability eligibility criteria for these students is the same as that for all students (based on federal and state regulations), school teams must view these students through the lens of twice exceptionality and not try to fit a square peg into a round hole because it simply will not fit. Indeed, these students are unique, and are in no way average, and so educators must look at them as individuals and use their knowledge of twice-exceptional students in order to reach and teach them to ensure their success in school.

REFERENCES

American Psychiatric Association. (2013). *Diagnostic and statistical manual of mental disorders* (5th ed.). Washington, DC: Author.

Assouline, S., Foley Nicpon, M., & Huber, D. (2006). The impact of vulnerabilities and strengths on the academic experiences of twice-exceptional students: A message to school counselors. *Professional School Counseling, 10*(1), 14–24.

Assouline, S., Foley Nicpon, M., & Whiteman, C. (2010). Cognitive and psychosocial characteristics of gifted students with specific learning disabilities. *Gifted Child Quarterly, 54,* 102–115.

Baum, S., Cooper, C., & Neu, T. (2001). Dual differentiation: An approach for meeting the needs of gifted students with learning disabilities. *Psychology in the Schools, 38,* 477–490.

Baum, S., & Owen, S. (2004). *To be gifted and learning disabled: Strategies for helping bright students with LD, ADHD, and more.* Waco, TX: Prufrock Press.

Barber, C., & Mueller, C. (2011). Social and self-perceptions of adolescents identified as gifted, learning disabled, and twice-exceptional. *Roeper Review, 33,* 109–120.

Brody, L., & Mills, C. (1997). Gifted children with learning disabilities: A review of the issues. *Journal of Learning Disabilities, 30,* 282–297.

Coleman, M. R. (2005). Academic strategies that work for gifted students with learning disabilities. *Teaching Exceptional Students, 38*(1), 28–32.

Council for Exceptional Children. (2007). *CEC's position on Response to Intervention: The unique role of special education and special educators.* Washington, DC: Author.

Foley Nicpon, M., Allmon, A., Sieck, B., & Stinson, R. (2011). Empirical investigation of twice-exceptionality: Where have we been and where are we going? *Gifted Child Quarterly, 55,* 3–17.

Foley Nicpon, M., Assouline, S., & Colangelo, N. (2013). Twice-exceptional learners: Who needs to know what? *Gifted Child Quarterly, 57,* 169–180.

Hughes, C. E. (2011). Twice-exceptional children: Twice the challenges, twice the joys. In J. A. Castellano & A. D. Frazier (Eds.), *Special populations in gifted education: Understanding our most able students from diverse backgrounds* (pp. 153–174). Waco, TX: Prufrock Press.

Individuals with Disabilities Education Improvement Act, Pub. Law 108-446 (December 3, 2004).

Mann, R. (2006). Effective teaching strategies for gifted/learning-disabled students with spatial strengths. *The Journal of Secondary Gifted Education, 17,* 112–122.

Montgomery County Public Schools. (2004). *Twice exceptional students: A guidebook for supporting the achievement of gifted students with special needs.* Rockville, MD: Author.

Montgomery County Public Schools. (2007). *Twice exceptional students: At a glance.* Rockville, MD: Author.

Morrison, W. F., & Rizza, M. G. (2007). Creating a toolkit for identifying twice-exceptional students. *Journal for the Education of the Gifted, 31,* 57–76.

National Association for Gifted Children. (2009). *Twice exceptionality* (NAGC Position Paper). Washington, DC: Author.

Pereles, D., Omdal, S., & Baldwin, L. (2009). Response to Intervention and twice-exceptional learners: A promising fit. *Gifted Child Today, 32*(3), 40–51.

Roberts, J., & Jolly, J. (2012). *A teacher's guide to working with children and families from diverse backgrounds.* Waco, TX: Prufrock Press.

Shevitz, B. R., Stemple, M., Barnes-Robinson, L., & Jeweler, S. (2011). *101 school success tools for smart kids with learning difficulties.* Waco, TX: Prufrock Press.

Silverman, L. (1993). *Counseling the gifted and talented.* Denver, CO: Love.

Silverman, L. (2002). *Upside-down brilliance: The visual-spatial learner.* Denver, CO: DeLeon.

Silverman, S. M., Kenworthy, L., & Weinfeld, R. (2014). *School success for kids with high-functioning autism.* Waco, TX: Prufrock Press.

The Association for the Gifted, Council for Exceptional Children, & National Association for Gifted Children. (2009). *Response to Intervention—A joint statement from the National Association for Gifted Children and CEC-TAG.* Retrieved from http://www.nagc. org/sites/default/files/Position%20Statement/RtI.pdf

Trail, B. (2011). *Twice-exceptional gifted children: Understanding, teaching, and counseling gifted students.* Waco, TX: Prufrock Press.

Weinfeld, R., Barnes-Robinson, L., Jeweler, S., & Shevitz, B. R. (2002). Academic programs for gifted and talented/learning disabled students. *Roeper Review, 24,* 226–233.

Weinfeld, R., Barnes-Robinson, L., Jeweler, S., & Shevitz, B. R. (2014). *Smart kids with learning difficulties: Overcoming obstacles and realizing potential* (2nd ed.). Waco, TX: Prufrock Press.

Yssel, N., Prater, M., & Smith, D. (2010). Finding the right fit for our twice-exceptional students in our schools. *Gifted Child Today, 33*(1), 55–61.

CHAPTER 6

Promising Practices From the Field: Identifying and Retaining Diverse Students in Gifted Programs: Voices of the Teachers of CLED Students

"All of us do not have equal talent, but all of us should have an equal opportunity to develop our talents."—John F. Kennedy

Why are educators continually challenged when it comes to the identification of gifted and high-potential students from culturally, linguistically, and/or ethnically diverse (CLED) populations, and what practices exist that are both promising and practical for identifying and retaining CLED diverse learners in gifted programs? Gifted and high-potential learners come from every socioeconomic, racial, and ethnic group, yet learners from diverse groups are historically underidentified as gifted and are underserved in gifted instruction and programming (Castellano & Frazier, 2011; Johnsen, 2011). As educators, we must continue to attempt to peel back the layers—to reflect on our practices, policies, and procedures—in an attempt to discover exactly why this disparity continues to exist and then work collaboratively (Roberts & Jolly, 2012) with all stakeholders to ensure that underserved students are recognized, supported, and shine in challenging instructional settings.

DOI: 10.4324/9781003235767-6

TEACHER PERSPECTIVES OF BEST PRACTICES

One way to try to better understand and analyze the obstacles that stand in the way of CLED students being identified as having unmet advanced academic needs, and not having access to programs and services for the gifted is to ask the practitioners in the field—the very teachers who have or are currently working with CLED gifted students. Because the majority of this book focuses on several groups of CLED students, we developed and sent out an online survey (see Appendix B) to teachers of gifted CLED students. The survey instrument contained 10 open-ended questions and was sent to more than 100 teachers of gifted CLED students across the United States in an attempt to capture their thinking about diverse gifted learners; 38 surveys were returned. They were completed anonymously so that these educators would feel completely free to express their ideas, perceptions, opinions, and experiences. Because of the anonymity of the responses, it was not possible to report the geographic location of the responders; however, a commonality they all shared is that they teach or have taught gifted CLED students in public schools for at least 5 years. Data were first reviewed for overall trends and patterns and then summarized based on findings.

The following synthesis of information is driven by the *voices* of teachers of gifted CLED students, examining the way these teachers of gifted CLED students view the issue of disproportionate identification and programming in the field, as well as promising practices for identifying and retaining CLED diverse students in gifted or challenging instructional settings.

OPPORTUNITY AND PERCEPTIONS

One area that surfaced in the survey was the notion of opportunity. Are diverse gifted learners given the opportunity to develop their gifts? Do lack of varied instructional practices and rigid curriculum guidelines stand in the way? Do teachers misunderstand the behaviors that surface in gifted diverse students? We asked: What are the academic/cognitive weaknesses that you find/found in diverse gifted learners? To what do you attribute this/these weakness/es? Teachers said:

- "Academic/cognitive 'weaknesses' may be stated more accurately as a condition of teaching and learning, not learner weakness. So-called learner weakness is the result of bad teaching—period! It is a result of learning environments (administration, teachers, systems, time, funding) that place learners at risk for learning. This is associated with concepts of appropriate access, opportunities for learning, and support. This is most evident when appropriate accommodations are not provided for them that reflect their strengths. Academic/cognitive weakness found in learners is because of the system, not of or in the learner."
- "Gifted [diverse] students frequently suffer because they are misunderstood. Their questioning of information is misinterpreted as being insolent."
- "Most of the students I have come across have a strong desire to learn but often get bored easily. When bored they start to slack off and in return look to the naked eye as struggling."

When analyzing the responses to this question, it was apparent that in many cases, the teachers did not actually answer the first question; several teachers did not identify a specific "weakness." Instead, the responses suggested that these teachers feel that the students are misunderstood and do not have proper academic support in place. It is refreshing to see that this group of teachers looks beyond perceived innate "weaknesses." We often find that a lack of understanding by the teachers leads to a lack of instructional opportunities for the students. Some teachers do hold incorrect perceptions about students from specific cultural or ethnic groups. These perceptions often include the belief that some of these children just cannot be successful, resulting in low expectations of the student. Both teachers and administrators can hold a mindset in which they believe that students can only go so far due to their innate intelligence, ability to persist, and/or ethnic background. Carol Dweck (2006), a psychology professor at Stanford University, referred to this as having a "fixed mindset" and this mindset frequently results in low achievement. If both teachers and students believe that students only have the ability

to go so far and that they cannot get "smarter," like a self-fulfilling proph-
ecy, that is exactly what will happen—students' progress will be limited.
Some responses from the teachers indicate just that:

- "The biggest problem with the students is the unwillingness to
commit to working hard."
- "The academic weaknesses frequently stem from lack of support
from home and intermittent periods of lack of persistence when
the content material becomes tough or is in an academic area
that is not their strength."

These responses reflect a belief system that will not allow a student to
demonstrate his or her potential. Even if it is demonstrated, would these
teachers recognize it and provide appropriately challenging experiences?

A school culture where educators, students, and parents believe that
intelligence is malleable and that all students can develop persistence and
motivation should be a goal in all schools. Dweck (2006) referred to this
as a "growth mindset." It is the belief that students can get "smarter" if
the teacher and the students truly believe that they can and are provided
with good instruction. When an educational community adopts this
belief, students from all backgrounds will be more willing to embrace
challenges. Ricci (2013) offered suggestions for teachers to help students
change their mindset, including teaching them about how the brain
works, introducing growth mindset terminology (and using it regularly
in the classroom), and providing challenging games and learning experiences to teach students perseverance. In summary, a promising and
practical strategy is to provide opportunities for students from diverse
backgrounds to participate in challenging, high-level curriculum and
instruction that includes the development of critical thinking processes
and to really believe that intelligence can be developed in all students.

PROFESSIONAL DEVELOPMENT

Some of the responses collected through the survey suggest that a few
of these teachers have had some training in gifted education and/or read
books or completed coursework on traditionally underserved gifted students. However, while not one of the survey questions, another pattern
that emerged through the survey is the lack of professional development

in the field. According to *Unlocking Emergent Talent: Supporting High Achievement of Low-Income, High-Ability Students,* "Our most vulnerable children are in classrooms with teachers who do not know how to spot talent or organize curriculum or instruction to nurture or develop it. Because of this lack of training, teachers underestimate the capabilities of gifted children" (Olszewski-Kubilius & Clarenbach, 2012, p. 9). Few undergraduate programs include coursework in gifted education and those that do rarely focus on diverse gifted learners. Therefore, any professional development must be obtained through district or school-based workshops. Educators can also pursue graduate coursework in the field if local institutions offer gifted coursework. One graduate student traveled 2 hours to Johns Hopkins University in Baltimore over several years to obtain a certificate in gifted education because the institutions of higher education in her area did not offer a gifted certificate program.

Do educators know what to look for to recognize potential in diverse student groups? Do they observe everyday behaviors in students, reflect on what this behavior might mean, and then respond to the student in an appropriate manor? We asked: Did you feel you needed any special skills or knowledge to identify the giftedness in or work with/teach your diverse gifted learners? If yes, please describe the special skills or knowledge needed to effectively work with diverse gifted learners. Teachers said:

- "I think my success has been greatly augmented by understanding the struggles of my students. Special training and other 'education in poverty' support have made me better able to serve these students. It is still very difficult to address the needs of the gifted student under significant stress or in great crisis. Problems of poverty, gang-related pressures, and deportation worries are just a few major factors that complicate the lives of my GT students beyond what we learn about as 'typical' for GT students."

- "I do believe I needed special training to work with these students and I pursued that training myself. I took a course on 2E Gifted with an expert in the field, and I also attended several workshops on gifted students from poverty. Students from these diverse groups have special needs as learners. Instruction for this group must include incorporating their intelligence and learning strengths in order to support any learning challenges they may have."

- "It has been helpful to learn that not all gifted behaviors appear 'pleasant.' Some of the traits can be expressed in disruptive/ behaviorally unacceptable ways. Also, in terms of products, some of the most 'off the wall' responses, if given a second look, make sense and are truly eye-opening."

- "It is imperative that all stakeholders continue to engage in opportunities to increase their knowledge and competencies about diversity in general and academic diversity as related to cultural diversity specifically."

Professional development opportunities must be made available (and perhaps mandated) that address the academic and social-emotional needs of diverse learners. The content of these sessions must address beliefs, expectations, and misconceptions about ethnicity, culture, and intelligence. Schools and systems must be willing to be reflective about current practices that inherently have bias based on cultural differences and the way they might value acceptable "behaviors" as a ticket to rigorous instructional opportunities. In summary, a promising and practical strategy is to analyze current professional development experiences for teachers to determine if any opportunities are available for teachers in the areas of identifying, instructing, supporting, and retaining students in advanced programming and instruction. Based on this analysis, schools can plan professional development opportunities for teachers through local workshops, university partnerships, and/or professional learning communities.

CULTURAL DIFFERENCES

Diverse gifted students often have some areas of struggle and these are usually what take priority. For those whose first language is not English, that struggle may occur in the area of language arts. Therefore, instruction for an English language learner may focus on learning to read and write English—his or her area of struggle. Because of the time devoted to the student's weakness, little time is devoted to the student's area of strength. The same applies to those students who are facing social/emotional issues due to poverty or lack of family support. We asked: What are the academic/cognitive strengths that you find/found in diverse gifted learners? Interestingly, many of the responses to this question ignored the identification of academic strengths and instead focused on the noncognitive/psychosocial areas of the students. Teachers said:

- "Gifted kids adapt and generate impressive strategies for coping. Cultural pressures and/or poverty give them a lot of opportunities to hone those skills. Unlike their academic peers in more 'traditional' environments, these students bring a higher degree of street smarts and adaptability to bear in their daily lives."

- "Like their 'non-diverse' counterparts, my GT students who face poverty or cultural diversity pressures experience erratic, sometimes out-of-sync development issues. I think they are better at working around their feelings. It seems that being 'out of step' has greater consequences in some environments than others, and the GT child can tune in to that."

- "They are aware of their differences. Those that come from a culture that doesn't value school successes try to hide their talents. They do genuinely enjoy finding peers who think like they think. Again, depending on the child . . . they are extremely social or they retreat into their own world."

These responses focus on the cultural and ethnic differences of students. A promising and practical strategy is to develop instructional sequences that focus on the "gifts" or strengths of the diverse gifted learner. Consideration of different cultural perspectives as well as consideration of students' interests should be imbedded in the curriculum. Instruction should be differentiated in order to meet the needs of the diverse learner. Help students relate to successful individuals in their ethnic group by providing positive role models through the use of bibliotherapy and community member mentoring.

CONCLUSION

In summary, although there is still much work to be done in the areas of nurturing, identifying, and retaining diverse students in advanced instructional settings, a good starting point is to reflect on and assess where your school/school district is with regard to the following four areas highlighted by teachers of CLED gifted students:

- *Opportunity*—Are our diverse learners provided opportunities to develop critical thinking and participate in challenging learning opportunities from a young age?
- *Perceptions*—Do educators hold an internal belief system that allows for diverse students to grow and embrace challenge?
- *Professional development*—What opportunities exist for professional growth in the area of diverse, high-potential learners?
- *Cultural differences*— Does assessment, curriculum, and instruction value cultural learning differences?

When these areas are considered and needed changes are made, more support will exist for recognizing and responding to the unique needs of gifted diverse learners. When it comes to educating gifted diverse learners, teachers say it best:

- "I love the stimulating atmosphere and their uniqueness makes me smile!"
- "They are a joy to see succeed! It inspires me to work specifically with this population and allow it to remain my passion! Changing lives in such a dramatic way!"
- "I love them and they teach me things every day."

Psychological science indicates the need for all students to be in a challenging instructional setting. Appropriate instruction, professional development, and support are required to develop a student's talents and abilities (Subotnik, Olszewski-Kubilius, & Worrell, 2012) to their full potential.

REFERENCES

Castellano, J. A., & Frazier, A. D. (Eds.). (2011). *Special populations in gifted education: Understanding our most able students from diverse backgrounds.* Waco, TX: Prufrock Press.

Dweck, C. (2006). *Mindset: The new psychology of success.* New York, NY: Random House.

Johnsen, S. K. (Ed.). (2011). *Identifying gifted students: A practical guide* (2nd ed.). Waco, TX: Prufrock Press.

Olszewski-Kubilius, P., & Clarenbach, J. (2012, October). *Unlocking emergent talent: Supporting high achievement of low-income, high-ability students.* National Association for Gifted Children. Retrieved from http://www.nagc.org/uploadedFiles/Conventions_and_Seminars/National_Research_Summit/Unlocking%20Emergent%20Talent%20FULL%20No-Tint.pdf

Ricci, M. C. (2013). *Mindsets in the classroom: Building a culture of success and student achievement in school.* Waco, TX: Prufrock Press.

Roberts, J., & Jolly, J. (2012). *A teacher's guide to working with children and families from diverse backgrounds.* Waco, TX: Prufrock Press.

Subotnik, R., Olszewski-Kubilius, P., & Worrell, F. (2012). A proposed direction forward for gifted education based on psychological science. *Gifted Child Quarterly, 56,* 176–188.

CHAPTER 7

One Perspective: The Challenges and Triumphs of a Former CLED Student in Programs for Gifted Middle School and High School Students

With the coming of brisk autumn mornings, my younger self anticipated the farewell to summer review textbooks from Costco. Changing leaves cued the end of my parents' never-ending brainteasers and the return to familiar classrooms at Happyvale Elementary School. Everything from the books in my desk to my homeroom teacher felt comfortable—too comfortable, I soon learned. Each year felt as predictable and narrow as the single file lines I stood in. The education that I once found undemanding and secure transformed the moment my fifth-grade teacher encouraged my mother to register me for testing for a gifted and talented (GT)/magnet middle school program. It wasn't until my enrollment in a GT/magnet middle school center for the highly gifted that I began experiencing education through a prism. Sixth to 12th grade (the period of time that I was in GT/magnet programs in middle school and high school) brought about ever-changing reflections of self, knowledge, and potential.

My kaleidoscopic fifth-grade classroom was like no other I would see in my next decade of education. The walls were adorned with colorful

 DOI: 10.4324/9781003235767-7

posters and the desks cradled students of colorful complexions. These are the students that would later ask why I didn't join them at the local middle school; the students who would write nothing more in my elementary school yearbook than a simple, "Good luck where you are going."

After one parent-teacher conference, my mother and my fifth-grade teacher became the first to foresee my destination. My mother soon became well-informed about GT/magnet programs and acquainted with the high-strung parents who trained their children to ace the tests for screening and selection. However, she was content with my performance and familiar with my neighborhood middle school. Unlike my fifth-grade teacher, she did not see an urgency to apply for the GT/magnet program; like me, she was comfortable. But with samples of my writing in one hand and my palm in the other, my mother supported my every stride toward the GT/magnet classrooms I would never forget. Ultimately, applying for the GT/magnet program was my own choice. My yearning for a program that offered endless reading and writing drove every minute of my preparation for the exams. Although I didn't anticipate the long bus rides and challenging transition ahead, I did anticipate the many students who would share my enthusiasm. I did anticipate a curriculum that would be like no other I had ever seen. As I turned in my grueling screening and selection exam and returned to my mom's embrace in the car, I did anticipate pride.

During my first week in the Humanities and Communications Magnet Program, I felt cradled by a newfound community. The early morning transport and distinct class rotation bonded our tight-knit group of 50 or so students. But the bond wasn't tight enough for me to disregard that I was one of only four African American students and that I didn't enroll from an elementary school GT/magnet program. Despite the nearly contagious enthusiasm of the teachers, I was quickly overwhelmed by what I felt I had to prove. The students from the GT/magnet program at Wonderful Elementary School appeared to be effortlessly prepared for our challenging classes. Familiar with the near-tears extent of my frustration with "impossible" math equations from Costco textbooks, my mother knew exactly how to console my academic insecurities. More importantly, my humanities teacher, Mrs. W., incessantly declared in each and every class, "Practice doesn't make perfect. Perfect practice makes perfect!"

Soon enough, the pressure shifted as I began to feel the weight of being "that Black girl" in the newly introduced "special" program at the minority-rich middle school. A double-consciousness emerged between my time in general P.E. classes and humanities magnet reading classes, an internal divide that was only eased by education itself. Although it was difficult to feel a sense of place, I never lost a sense of purpose. From the moment my fifth-grade teacher advocated for my enrollment in the GT/magnet middle school program, to the moment I boarded the buses for extraordinary humanities field trips I experienced in the program, I took pride in my bettered self. The solidarity among the few students of color in the GT/magnet program was quiet but unquestionable. We became all too familiar with the sneers for "acting White" by virtue of our quickly blossoming enthusiasm for the GT/magnet program. But it was that enthusiasm that brought about my sense of place; it was the solidarity that emerged among our passionate community of students, parents, and teachers that made me appreciate the basis of my belonging.

By eighth grade, the season for applications for high school GT/magnet programs once again blossomed with pressure for recommendations and nerves for testing. After 3 years of phenomenal interdisciplinary projects, field trips, teachers, and friendships in the GT/magnet middle school program, the decision to apply for a GT/magnet high school program felt natural. My closest friends accompanied me to Pride High School, a challenging 4 years of bus rides that I didn't realize could get any longer and expectations that I never knew could be so high. A community once again emerged among the humanities students. The bond among students of color, however, was of a different nature, as Pride High School was located at the center of a predominantly White, rural town. Invited to everything from minority scholarships to NAACP student groups, my identity as a student and as an African American intersected more than ever. Yet my experiences from fifth grade until then could never prepare me for the numbing moment a student said, "You got into that college because you're Black!"

At that point, the rollercoaster of pride and insecurity felt never-ending. It's a rollercoaster ridden by countless culturally, linguistically, and ethnically diverse students across the country. It is a rollercoaster that shows little mercy for the struggles to make sense of capability, potential, and selfhood. In those spheres, advocacy is painfully underestimated. Many students are not privileged to have the academic support I was granted in the moment my fifth-grade teacher held a conference with my mother. Too many students are not pushed to explore beyond the comfort of what they know and only feel discomfort in who they are. Discomfort should only breed from the unforgettable challenges to our intellectual inhibitions. As CLED students experience the unexpected and learn the unexplored, they deserve every ounce of encouragement from teachers, friends, and communities who will embrace their passions and their complexions.

CHAPTER 8

Closing Words

"Outstanding talents are present in children from all cultural groups, across all economic strata, and in all areas of human endeavor."—U.S. Department of Education (1994) *National Excellence* report

Gifted learners are diverse. All gifted learners have the right to reach their academic potential and to be fully prepared to compete in and contribute to a more globalized world. However, historically, students who are culturally, linguistically, and/or ethnically diverse and/or students in some categories of disability have been underidentified as gifted and underrepresented in gifted programs. Why? Although limited, the research is replete with reasons for this longstanding, persistent issue in gifted education in America. The reasons cited include: limitations of identification tools; biased assessments; a hyper focus on academic achievement or traditional measures of success; lack of rigorous instructional opportunities through a high-quality curriculum; low teacher expectations; cultural differences; institutional practices, racism, and biases; a focus on deficits rather than the strengths students possess; a lack of targeted professional development for teachers and administrators; and lack of parent engagement and knowledge about gifted identification processes, programs, and services. These factors have led to the overidentification and provisioning of services for gifted learners from the majority/mainstream culture and not those across diverse student groups.

 DOI: 10.4324/9781003235767-8

It is the obligation of every educator to work aggressively to reverse these emblems of what have become two of our nation's greatest failures: the underidentification of diverse gifted learners and their underrepresentation in gifted programs. Recommendations for eradicating underidentification and underrepresentation among diverse gifted learners include (Ford, 2011):

- acknowledge that the characteristics of gifted students may look different based on cultural filters;
- use multiple measures when identifying diverse students, such as portfolios, interviews, personal recommendations, and performance assessments;
- foster opportunities for effective support for diverse students through options such as professional, community, or peer mentors;
- develop curriculum and learning activities that take into consideration cultural perspectives and student interests or preferences, differentiating the learning to respond to individual needs of the diverse gifted learner;
- create staff development opportunities that address the academic and affective needs of diverse gifted students and open collective staff understanding by addressing misconceptions and biases based on differences in cultural perspectives; and
- identify and modify school practices that present a bias against the diverse gifted learner; these may include practices related to student placement procedures, textbook selection, choice of curriculum content, instructional practices, and student awards and recommendations.

If America is truly going to ensure that no child is left behind, educators must embrace diversity, accept the fact that giftedness manifests itself differently in different groups, and acknowledge that giftedness is not found in only one group. Indeed, diverse gifted learners can be found in *every* cultural, racial, linguistic, and ethnic group regardless of gender, geographic location, disability, or socioeconomic status. Additionally, educators must subscribe to the fact that giftedness manifests through a variety of behaviors—not a limited few; that giftedness that manifests in one area (i.e., leadership) is just as important as giftedness that manifests in another area (i.e., math); and that giftedness in one domain can be an indicator of or springboard to the presence of giftedness in another area. For example, if a child demonstrates a great strength/giftedness in the ability to express him or herself verbally, with the right opportunities and support, giftedness in the area of expressive writing may also surface. Moreover, educators entrusted to provide all students with a world-class education must embrace the fact that intelligence is a broad concept that incorporates a wide range of human abilities. Intelligence is more than just an IQ score, one data point, or how well one can read, write, solve math problems, or speak Standard American English. If diverse gifted learners are to reach their full potential and are prepared to successfully contribute to and compete in the more globalized workforce of the 21st century, it is incumbent upon educators, parents, policy makers, and the general public to increase their efforts to implement what we already know works to ensure the needs of CLED and twice-exceptional learners are met and that they are abundantly identified as gifted and amply represented and retained in gifted programs and services.

REFERENCES

Ford, D. Y. (2011). *Reversing underachievement among gifted Black students* (2nd ed.). Waco, TX: Prufrock Press.

U.S. Department of Education, Office of Educational Research. (1994). *National excellence: A case for developing America's talent.* Washington, DC: U.S. Government Printing Office.

APPENDIX A

Resources

MYTHS ABOUT GIFTED EDUCATION

Myth	Reality
Global giftedness	More often than not, children are unevenly gifted, often being especially gifted in one area. It's not uncommon to find them quite gifted in a specific area, but average or learning disabled in another.
Talented, but not gifted	Artistically or athletically talented children exhibit many of the same characteristics of academically gifted students.
Exceptional IQ	IQ tests measure a narrow range of human abilities, primarily facility with language and numbers, which does not provide evidence of nonacademic areas of giftedness, such as art or music.
Biology (nature) vs. environment (nurture)	Giftedness is not entirely inborn. The environment offers many powerful influences on the development of gifts.
Environment (nurture) vs. biology (nature)	The powerful role of biology determines if any predisposition of a gift exists in which the environment can develop.
The driving parent	A gifted child tends to require an unusual degree of investment and involvement from the parents, but only for the development of their gift (An overzealous parent cannot create a gifted child).
Glowing with psychological health	Gifted children often face ridicule and taunts from their peers. Gifted children are often socially isolated and unhappy, unless they are fortunate enough to find others like themselves.

Myth	Reality
All children are gifted	All children have areas of strengths and all children have a strong potential to learn, however, not all children have exceptional academic gifts that require additional or different support in school.
Gifted children become eminent adults	Giftedness is usually seen as synonymous with high IQ and high creativity, however, many gifted children burn out and move on to other areas of interest. Over and above level of ability, important roles are played by personality, motivation, the family environment, opportunity, and chance.

Note. From *Gifted children: Myths and realities* by E. Winner, 1996, New York, NY: Basic Books. Copyright 1996 Basic Books. Reprinted with permission.

CHARACTERISTICS OF CULTURALLY, LINGUISTICALLY, AND/OR ETHNICALLY DIVERSE (CLED) GIFTED LEARNERS: AN OBSERVATION, DATA COLLECTION, AND INSTRUCTIONAL DECISION-MAKING TOOL

Directions: CLED students are underrepresented and underserved in gifted programs and services. Research indicates that educators frequently do not have the knowledge about the gifted characteristics of this population. The chart below lists research-based observable behaviors that are traditionally not considered for identification of gifted CLED students. Educators should review this document in order to better advocate for students who demonstrate some or all of these characteristics of giftedness. Educators should list the names of the students who demonstrate these characteristics in the first blank column. The second blank column can be used to collect additional observations and notes. Students who exhibit several of these behaviors should be flagged and considered along with other data points/measures for further consideration for GT identification and/or challenging instructional opportunities.

Characteristics of Gifted Students	Characteristics of CLED Gifted Students	Students' Names	Observation Notes	Recommendations/ Instructional Implications
Inquisitive: Searches for significance and meaning	Quick to note lack of relevance in assignments, rules, etc. May question or resist authority/adults Asks more provocative questions about the cause of things Asks challenging questions that could be perceived as critical or judgmental Other: _____			
Use of Language: Advanced, large vocabulary; verbal proficiency	Can use words to manipulate or present double messages Sometimes uses words and language considered inappropriate in school settings Talkative Other: _____			
Creative: inventive, innovative, divergent thinkers	Dislikes structure, routine Dares to be different; risk taker; enjoys challenges Questions, explores, and/or experiments verbally or nonverbally Sees things that others do not, resourceful, sees many alternatives Displays sophisticated humor such as puns/double meanings Other: _____			
Energetic: High Energy, Lively, Verve	Frustrated and bored by inactivity Highly engaged during active learning and experiential learning Physical energy Other: _____			
Varied and Diverse Interests	Willing to take risks May not show strengths in one area Attention easily diverted Intense curiosity about many things May interrupt to pursue own interests Other: _____			

Characteristics of Gifted Students	Characteristics of CLED Gifted Students	Students' Names	Observation Notes	Recommendations/ Instructional Implications
Heightened Sensitivity	Defensive or stubborn Powerful emotions Self-centered/narrow minded Confronts rather than accepts inequities Other: _____			
Leadership	Influences and persuades others, positively or negatively Organizes a group in work or play to carry out a plan of action Other: _____			
Linguistically: learns quickly/easily	Attempts to communicate in English most of the time Demonstrates the ability to make connections to their prior learning Does not rely on student translator to communicate Creatively uses language and nonverbal forms of communication to express ideas and make connections to conceptual knowledge Shows the ability to transition among languages Other: _____			
Problem Solving	Can solve problems in situations that are not English dependent (e.g., tangrams, numbers/math, classification, etc.) Other: _____			

Adapted from Brulles, Castellano, and Laing (2011); Castellano (2002); and Ford (2003).

TRAITS OF GIFTEDNESS: A NONBIASED PROFILE

Note. A student does not have to show all 12 traits to be considered gifted.

Characteristic/ Attribute	Evidence	Students May . . .
DRIVE/INCENTIVE	Motivation to learn	• Demonstrate persistence in pursuing or completing self-selected activities in school or after school (may be culturally influenced) • Aspire to achieve something significant, to be somebody, to do something impactful
INTERESTS	Strong and sometimes uncommon interest(s)	• Have compelling uncommon, rare, or advanced interests • Take the initiative; be a self-starter • Engage in a task well beyond the time other students can attend to a task/ activity
COMMUNICATION SKILLS	Highly expressive with words, numbers, or symbols	• Have an uncommon ability to communicate in a variety of ways (i.e., verbally, nonverbally, physically, artistically, or symbolically) • Utilize an abundance of appropriate examples, illustrations, or elaborations
PROBLEM-SOLVING SKILLS	Inventive processes for identifying and resolving problems	• Demonstrate an uncommon ability to create an organized/methodical solution to a problem • Adjust the problem-solving process if it's not working • Be highly creative and inventive creating new strategies and generating new ideas
MEMORY	Depth of knowledgeable about a variety of topics	• Be well versed on a variety topics • Require few repetitions for mastery • Posses a broad range of information about a wide variety topics • Be detail oriented • Be able to easily grasp and handle a variety of information

Characteristic/ Attribute	Evidence	Students May . . .
INQUISITIVE/CURIOUS	Questions, experiments, explores	• Asks uncommon questions for age • Easily engage with ideas • Demonstrate extensive investigative behaviors for eliciting information about materials, devices, or situations
INSIGHT	Quickly grasps new concepts and ideas; makes connections for deeper meaning and understanding	• Possess an exceptional ability to draw inferences • Be a good risk-taker • Be intensely observant • Have a heightened capacity for seeing unusual and diverse relationships • Have the ability to integrate ideas, information and multiple disciplines
IMAGINATION/CREATIVITY	Produces many ideas; flexible thinking; highly original	• Be exceptionally imaginative when using routine, everyday materials; • Be keenly observant and aware • Have diverse and sometimes silly ideas • Be very inquisitive
HUMOR	Advanced sense of humor (expressive, receptive and perceptive)	• Possess a keen sense of humor that may be gentle or harsh • Possess a high "emotional IQ" • Possess an uncommon depth of emotional understanding • Amenable to different experiences • Unusual sensory awareness
INTENSE "OVEREXCITABILITIES"	Degree of reactions, responses, behaviors	• Develop strong attachments to people, places, and things (powerful emotions) • Be sympathetic to others; but not themselves • Be highly self-critical and/or anxious • Desire intellectual stimulation • Evoke strong emotional response from certain sensory experiences evoke strong responses • Develop a strong attachment to people, places, things, and events • Engage in constant or repetitive movement or gesturing • Have intense imagination • Find enjoyment in creative experiences

Characteristic/ Attribute	Evidence	Students May ...
REASONING 	Reasons and evaluates situations logically	• Think logically • Think critically • Think analytically • Consider many points of view • Make generalizations • Utilize metaphors and analogies
SENSITIVE 	Heightened and intense emotions and emotional responses to events and experiences	• Possess a strong sense of compassion • Possess an unusual sense of social justice and fairness • Be empathetic • Have a strong sense of ethical awareness • Demonstrate unique ("different") social behaviors • Worry unnecessarily ("turn molehills into mountains") • Be overly self-critical • Overreact or be overly critical of others

Note. From Colorado State Department of Education (n.d.).

CHARACTERISTICS OF GIFTED STUDENTS WITH AND WITHOUT DISABILITIES

Characteristics of Gifted Students Without Learning Difficulties	Characteristics of Gifted Students With Learning Difficulties	Observations/Notes
Ability to learn basic skills quickly and easily and retain information with less repetition	Often struggle to learn basic skills; need to learn compensatory strategies in order to acquire basic skills and information	
High verbal ability	High verbal ability but extreme difficulty in written language area; may use language in inappropriate ways and at inappropriate times	
Early reading ability	Frequently have reading problems	
Keen powers of observation	Strong observation skills but often have deficits in memory skills	
Strong critical thinking, problem-solving, and decision-making skills	Excel in solving real-world problems; outstanding critical thinking and decision-making skills; often independently develop compensatory skills	
Long attention span; persistent, intense concentration	Frequently have attention problems but may concentrate for long periods in areas of interest	
Questioning attitudes	Strong questioning attitudes; may appear disrespectful when questioning information and facts presented by teacher	

Characteristics of Gifted Students Without Learning Difficulties	Characteristics of Gifted Students With Learning Difficulties	Observations/Notes
Creative in the generation of thoughts, ideas, actions; innovative	Unusual imagination; frequently generate original and at times rather bizarre ideas; extremely divergent in thought; may appear to daydream when generating ideas	
Take risks	Often unwilling to take risks with regard to academics; take risks in nonschool areas without consideration of consequences	
Unusual, often highly developed sense of humor	Humor may be used to divert attention from school failure; may use humor to make fun of peers or to avoid trouble	
May mature at different rates than age peers	Sometimes appear immature because they may use anger, crying, withdrawal, and other emotions to express feelings and to deal with difficulties	
Sense of independence	Require frequent teacher support and feedback in weakness areas; highly independent in other areas; often appear to be extremely stubborn and inflexible	
Sensitive	Sensitive regarding weaknesses; highly critical of self and others including teachers; can express concerns about the feelings of others even while engaging in antisocial behavior	

Characteristics of Gifted Students Without Learning Difficulties	Characteristics of Gifted Students With Learning Difficulties	Observations/Notes
May not be accepted by other children and may feel isolated	May not be accepted by other children and may feel isolated; may be perceived as loners because they do not fit the typical model for either a gifted or a learning disabled student; sometimes have difficulty being accepted by peers due to poor social skills	
Exhibit leadership ability	Exhibit leadership ability; often serve as leaders among the more nontraditional students; demonstrate strong streetwise behavior; the difficulties may interfere with the ability to exercise leadership skills	
Wide range of interests	Wide range of interests but are limited in pursuing them due to learning problems	
Very focused interests (i.e., a passion about certain topics to the exclusion of others)	Very focused interests (i.e., a passion about certain topics to the exclusion of others) often not related to school subjects	

Note. From *101 School Success Tools for Smart Kids With Learning Difficulties* (pp. 11–13) by B. R. Shevitz, M. Stemple, L. Barnes-Robinson, and S. Jeweler, 2011, New York, NY: Taylor & Francis. Copyright 2011 Taylor & Francis. Reprinted with permission.

APPENDIX A REFERENCES

Brulles, D., Castellano, J. A., & Laing, P. C. (2011). Identifying and enfranchising gifted English language learners. In J. A. Castellano & A. D. Frazier (Eds.), *Special populations in gifted education: Understanding our most able students from diverse backgrounds* (pp. 305–313). Waco, TX: Prufrock Press.

Castellano, J. A. (2002). *Special populations in gifted education: Working with diverse gifted learners.* Boston, MA: Allyn & Bacon.

Colorado State Department of Education. (n.d.). *Twelve traits of giftedness: A non-biased profile.* Retrieved from http://www.cde.state.co.us/sites/default/files/documents/gt/download/pdf/twelve_traits_of_giftedness_cld.pdf

Ford, D. Y. (2003). Equity and excellence: Culturally diverse students in gifted education. In N. Colangelo & G. A. Davis (Eds.), *Handbook of gifted education* (3rd ed., pp. 506–520). Boston, MA: Allyn & Bacon.

Shevitz, B. R., Stemple, M., Barnes-Robinson, L., & Jeweler, S. (2011). *101 school success tools for smart kids with learning difficulties.* Waco, TX: Prufrock Press.

Winner, E. (1996). *Gifted children: Myths and realities.* New York, NY: Basic Books.

APPENDIX B

Diverse Gifted Learners: Teacher Survey Protocol

SURVEY EMAIL COVER LETTER

Dear _____,

I am working with colleagues in various parts of the United States to create a document that will help shed light on the national problem of the underrepresentation of diverse students in classes and programs for the gifted. This project is for The Association of the Gifted (TAG), which is a division of the Council for Exceptional Children (CEC). We are surveying past and current teachers of diverse gifted learners in order to gain their perspective on what must be done to identify, attract, and retain diverse gifted learners in advanced level classes and programs. Attached is the brief survey. It is totally anonymous. Names, school districts, and other identifying information will not be referenced in the final document. Additionally, please note that while aligned to my passion for gifted education, this work is outside of the work I do for _____ (INSERT SCHOOL DISTRICT).

Thank you for your support and please don't hesitate to contact me should you have any questions or need additional information.

Sincerely,

_____

DIVERSE GIFTED LEARNERS: TEACHER SURVEY QUESTIONS

- How long have you taught/did you teach diverse gifted learners?
- Are there any special learning characteristics (e.g., learning styles) you found in the diverse gifted learners you serve/served? Please elaborate.
- Did you feel you needed any special skills or knowledge to identify the giftedness in or work with/teach your diverse gifted learners?
- What are the academic/cognitive strengths that you find/found in diverse gifted learners?
- What are the academic/cognitive weaknesses that you find/found in diverse gifted learners? To what do you attribute this/these weakness/es?
- How do you characterize diverse gifted learners' social-emotional development?
- Have you ever observed/interacted with your diverse gifted learners outside of the classroom? If so, what, if any, insights did you gain about your diverse gifted learners that had implications for their schooling from that/those experience/s?
- What do you think should be/can be done to attract and retain more diverse gifted learners in advanced level classes/programs?
- As a teacher of the gifted, do you and/or your school do anything specifically to retain diverse gifted learners in your advanced level classes/programs?
- Are there any additional things you want to share about diverse gifted learners?

About the Authors

Monique Felder, Ph.D., is the former Director of the Division of Accelerated and Enriched Instruction for Montgomery County Public Schools (MCPS) in Maryland. Dr. Felder supervised instructional specialists and coordinated and supported accelerated and enriched instruction/gifted and talented programs and services for K–12, including teacher professional development. Other positions held in MCPS include director of the Interventions Network, supervisor, principal, and classroom teacher. Dr. Felder was elected to the CEC-The Association for the Gifted (TAG) board of directors and she served on the Maryland State Department of Education's Gifted and Talented Advisory Board. Currently, Dr. Felder is the Coordinating Supervisor for the Deputy Superintendent for Teaching and Learning for Prince George's County Public Schools in Maryland. She is also a faculty associate at McDaniel College where she teaches graduate level courses in curriculum and instruction. Additionally, Dr. Felder coordinates the Institute for Educational Leadership's flagship leadership program—Education Policy and Fellowship Program in Washington, DC. Dr. Felder holds a bachelor's degree in education with a specialization in early childhood education from York College in New York City; a master's degree in education with a concentration in elementary mathematics and science and a certificate in administration and supervision from Johns Hopkins University; and a Ph.D. in educational leadership and policy studies from Virginia Tech. In 2014, Dr. Felder earned a graduate certificate in equity and excellence in education from McDaniel College. She has presented locally, nationally, and internationally on a variety of topics in education.

Gloria Taradash, Ph.D., holds a bachelor's degree in African American studies, a master's degree in secondary education, and a Ph.D. in special education with an emphasis on gifted minorities and parents. She has dedicated her focus to service, working on the board of directors of the National Association for Gifted Children and serving as president of the Special Populations Division. For the Council for Exceptional Children (CEC), she served as president of The Association for the Gifted (TAG) and the Division for Culturally and Linguistically Diverse Exceptional Learners (DDEL) and on the board of directors of the Black Caucus of Special Educators. She has served on many standing committees where she worked to increase diversity in positions of leadership in CEC. Dr. Taradash has presented at local, state, national, and international conferences on issues of gifted diversity and families. She has served on the board of reviewers for the *Journal for the Education of the Gifted, Gifted Child Quarterly,* and the *Journal of Secondary Gifted Education.* During Dr. Taradash's terms as president of the New Mexico Association for the Gifted and the Albuquerque Association for the Gifted and Talented, she organized parent groups for gifted children across the state of New Mexico. While serving as a governor's appointee to the Judicial Standards Commission, she was elected vice-chair throughout her 9-year term.

Elise Antoine, M.Ed., holds a bachelor's degree in elementary education, a master's degree in guidance and counseling, and a post-master's certificate in administration and supervision. Antoine has been an educator in Montgomery County Public Schools (MCPS) in Maryland for 15 years. Her classroom experiences include teaching in diverse Title I schools and serving as a mentor teacher in the elementary Center Program for the Highly Gifted. She is currently an instructional specialist and curriculum developer in the Office of Curriculum and Instructional Programs. She is coauthor of the elementary Center Program for the Highly Gifted interdisciplinary curriculum and provides ongoing professional development and program support across multiple sites. In 2011, Antoine was awarded Teacher as Leader in Gifted Education by the Maryland State Advisory Council on Gifted and Talented Education. She serves on the steering committee for the Maryland State Conference on Gifted and

Talented Education and has presented at local, state, and regional conferences on issues related to addressing the needs of highly able students and equitable access to enrichment and acceleration. She is completing her second term on the Maryland State Department of Education Advisory Council for Gifted and Talented Education, where she serves as chair of the Programs and Services subcommittee.

Mary Cay Ricci, M.Ed., is an independent education consultant and speaker. She was previously the Coordinator of Gifted and Talented Education for Baltimore County Public Schools, MD, and an instructional specialist in the Division of Enriched and Accelerated Instruction for Montgomery County Public Schools, MD. Ricci holds a master's degree that includes certification in gifted and talented education and administration and supervision from Johns Hopkins University, where she is currently a faculty associate in the Graduate School of Education. She completed her undergraduate degree in elementary education at Mercyhurst University. Ricci has experience as an elementary and middle school teacher. She also serves on the CEC-TAG board of directors and the Maryland State Department of Education's Gifted and Talented Advisory Board. She is the author of the best-selling book, *Mindsets in the Classroom: Building a Culture of Success and Student Achievement in Schools* published by Prufrock Press.

Marisa Stemple, M.Ed., has spent her entire career in education within Maryland's Montgomery County Public Schools working with and on behalf of bright students with learning disabilities. She began in 1997 as a teacher of gifted and talented/learning disabled (GT/LD) students at Colonel E. Brooke Lee Middle School where she taught and cotaught English, reading, science, and resource to twice-exceptional students in grades 6–8. In addition, for several years she served as the twice-exceptional/GT/LD coordinator for the program at Lee. In 2004–2005, she became the instructional specialist for GT/LD programs and services and is responsible for coordinating MCPS's nationally recognized GT/LD programs. Stemple also provides consultation and professional development to MCPS schools and teachers on behalf of twice-exceptional students. She serves as a resource for parents and works closely with the GT/LD Network, a parent advocacy group from the GT/LD community, to increase awareness and understanding of twice-exceptional students, programs, and services in MCPS. She has presented at local, state, and national conferences on gifted education. She received her bachelor's degree in special education and a master's degree in learning disabilities from the University of Maryland at College Park. She received a certificate in administration and supervision as well as a graduate certificate in gifted education from Johns Hopkins University. Additionally, Stemple is one of the coauthors of *101 School Success Tools for Smart Kids With Learning Difficulties* published by Prufrock Press.

Michelle Byamugisha is a postgraduate student at London School of Economics and Political Science and a Northwestern University alum. She was born and raised in Maryland into a family of Ugandan descent. At Northwestern, Byamugisha served as President of the African Students Association and today studies media, communication, and development. She enjoys travel, creative nonfiction writing, and the studies of community engagement and diaspora.